T0243237

The T in LGBT

The T in LGBT

EVERYTHING YOU NEED TO KNOW ABOUT BEING TRANS

JAMIE RAINES

Published by Sourcebooks
P.O. Box 4410, Naperville, Illinois 60567-4410
(630) 961-3900
sourcebooks.com

Originally published in 2023 in Great Britain by Vermilion,
an imprint of Ebury Publishing. Vermilion is part of the
Penguin Random House group of companies whose addresses
can be found at global.penguinrandomhouse.com

Cataloging-in-Publication Data is on file with the Library of Congress.

Printed and bound in the United States of America.
MA 10 9 8 7 6 5 4 3 2 1

I would like to dedicate this book to the trans community. This book is primarily for you, and made possible by you.

I'd also like to dedicate this book to my wife, Shaaba, and to my parents, who have supported me every step of the way.

Thank you.

Contents

HEY, I'M JAMIE.
WELCOME TO MY BOOK

Hey, my name's Jamie, and I'm trans. Thanks for picking up my guide on all things transgender. I called this guide *The T in LGBT* because - spoiler - that is actually how I came out to someone very close to me.

Just like the title reflects, this book is a combination of my personal stories and experiences mixed with practical and factual advice about what being trans is, the steps that might be involved to live as your true self and how to navigate as a trans person within society.

This guide also includes the voices of many others, mostly other trans people of varying identities, but allies too.

There's no one way of being trans, and no right or wrong way to transition.

That's why this guide showcases many different voices and paths of transitioning.

But in terms of my contributions, why should you listen to me?

Who Am I?

Well, firstly, I'm trans – surprise! Ha-ha. I talk about it a lot in videos that I put online as a full-time content creator. My channel, Jammidodger, is all about transitioning, being trans, breaking down transphobia and homophobia and a few other topics that I think people might find interesting (and that I do, too). My main aim is to educate through entertainment (you're learning, but you don't know it!), but also to give people a safe space, provide helpful info about being trans and hopefully to help other trans people feel a little less alone.

I first started making videos when I was 17 in 2011, nearly a year after I figured out I was trans myself, and just before I started taking hormones. (How has it been over a decade already?!) My main aim was to document my personal transition and the physical changes that testosterone would cause. I took a photo of my face every day for a good four years because I really wanted to be able to look back and notice any changes in my facial structure and watch my facial hair coming in (which required a lot of patience, as it turned out!).

I also had a secondary idea of maybe, possibly, helping at least one other trans person going through their journey in the UK. YouTube had been a lifeline of hope for me when I was figuring out my 'transness' (that's definitely not a word, but hey-ho). There were only three trans people I could find online sharing their stories, and they were all from the United States. Yes, I felt less alone watching them, but the process of transitioning and accessing healthcare and resources can be very different depending on where you are in the world, and I was still none the wiser about what I actually needed to do!

I knew that once I did figure it out I wanted to share my findings to help others, and that's how my channel was born. (You can thank my wife, Shaaba, for that name. She used to call me 'Dodger' because 'Jamie' sounds like 'Jammie'.) I remember my first video reaching 98 views, and I was so nervous about how many people that was. My heart would race at each new comment that came in and I nearly took it down! I'm very glad I didn't, though. Being a creator and raising awareness about trans issues online has become my full-time job, and I recently hit a milestone of reaching 1 million subscribers on the Jammidodger channel – younger Jamie would never have believed it!

When I first started the channel, almost all of the videos I made were about my personal experiences of transitioning. The changes I noticed on testosterone, how to bind safely, dealing with dysphoria, things like that. I thought this would be particularly useful when I went through big and personal trans journey 'milestones', but I see my transition as being complete now. Apart from the hair that is slowly taking over my entire body (!), there's not that much to personally talk about anymore.

In December 2019 I made a video that was about my transition, from start to finish, to kind of round off that chapter of my life. It felt like a very special video to make, and I think it will always be one of my favourites. I now use my platform to talk about the trans experience more generally, often looking at stories and memes from other people.

FEB 2011

SEP 2011

AUG 2011

AUG 2012

JAN 2012

JAN 2018

NOV 2019

I also try to share other aspects of my life that aren't just to do with being trans, because I'm so much more than that one part of my identity. I'm a doctoral researcher; I'm a husband to my best friend, Shaaba; I'm a cat-dad to two balls of fluff called Apollo and Prawn; I'm a dinosaur geek and I would buy ALL the Lego sets if I had the space for them (but don't tell Shaaba, she'd never allow it!); I'm a fashion enthusiast; I'm a Coca-Cola fiend; I'm a huge bookworm; and I'm a writer. I've created short stories and poems for as long as I can remember being able to write. Younger me would be amazed and ridiculously excited that I've actually written a whole book! Oh my gosh.

Did you catch my sneaky mention of being a doctoral researcher above? I'm not trying to brag: my PhD in psychology was focused on the development and wellbeing of transgender people, so I've done a lot of research to make this guide helpful. Technically that makes me a doctor, but I can't help with diagnosing a rash – though I can tell you if something is statistically significant!

I hope my experience as a trans person, a trans creator, a doctoral researcher and an LGBT+ advocate assures you that I know my shit.

So, Who Are You?

Maybe you're very sure how to answer that question, or maybe you're still trying to figure it out. Whether you're questioning, starting to figure things out or have already begun your transition, this guide is for you.

This book is also for you if you're an ally, or have a trans loved one who's made you want to learn more. Even if you're unaccepting or not comfortable about trans people, I hope this guide proves to be of some value to you.

Everyone is welcome.
That's how it should always be.

HOW TO USE THIS BOOK

Maybe as a doorstop, or as something to pop your phone stand on to get that perfect selfie height? I hope you'll actually read this too, ha-ha, and I want to give you some guidance on how best to do that, plus a little key to some special elements you'll find.

- There's no particular order you should read this book in. You can skip about between the topics that you need advice or info on, or you can read it cover to cover with each chapter in order. It's totally up to you.

- As you might imagine, there will be frank discussion around gender dysphoria, surgeries, genitals, transphobia, so only dive into topics you feel up for. There might be some sections you find tricky to read through depending on your state of mind. I for one would not be able to read about dysphoria if I was feeling particularly dysphoric. I've provided a quick overview at the beginning of each chapter of what's going to be covered, and some of them have trigger warnings. Look out for these if you feel you need to.

- ☆ **Top Tip:** Fellow fantastic trans people, keep an eye out for these sections throughout this book that might provide little hacks to make your journey of self-love and understanding easier.

- 💜 **For the Allies:** Awesome allies, keep an eye out for these sections throughout this book for little tips on how to best support a trans loved one. You may note that some of these are signed ' – Shaaba', and that's because my gorgeous wife wrote these sections! She's been the best ally for me and has some great best practices to share.

- While it's true that no single trans journey is the same, a lot of trans advice applies to everyone in the community – trans men, trans women and non-binary people alike. A good 80 per cent of this book applies to everyone, but for specific topics, like aspects of socially transitioning (such as packing or tucking), or surgeries (such as double mastectomy or breast augmentation), I've highlighted subheadings like this:

- You'll also see text boxes. These will feature invaluable insight from other contributors – either longer extracts from one person in particular, or shorter quotes from several people in response to a question (a random sample of trans people from around the world answered these – a huge thank-you to everybody who took part!). It should be clear when the information provided is from a contributor instead of me. ☆ **Top Tip:** You might find it useful to answer these questions yourself as little exercises to help you under-stand your identity and journey better (look at me being all helpful already).

- Finally, you might see footnotes at the bottom of some pages, which will look a bit like this: 'Title of Paper' (Year), Authors, *Publication*. These are academic sources, and you can search for them online to find the full papers. As a doctoral graduate, it felt important to highlight some of the research to support facts that are frequently disputed by transphobes, or miscom-municated in ways that damage the trans community. We don't need science to know who we are, but I wanted to equip you with some credible sources to share with others if you ever feel you need to.

When you're feeling ready, let's go!

A Glossary of Sorts:
Putting It All on the Table

AFAB Shorthand for 'assigned female at birth' and typically used when discussing trans masculine people (trans men and AFAB non-binary people).

AMAB Shorthand for 'assigned male at birth' and typically used when discussing trans feminine people (trans women and AMAB non-binary people).

Assigned sex at birth Refers to the sex a person was assigned at birth – that's a terrible definition, isn't it? It's basically the sex label you were given when you were born based on the appearance of your genitals. People born with a penis are AMAB and people born with a vagina are AFAB.

Baby trans The unofficial term for people who have just figured out they're trans/are in the very early stages of their transition.

Birthname/deadname Refers to the name trans people had before they transitioned. Birthnames can be a difficult topic for trans people and cause a lot of dysphoria.

Bottom surgery No, it's not a surgery of the butt. It's the colloquial term used to refer to genital surgery that trans people may undergo, including phalloplasty, metoidioplasty and vaginoplasty. We'll look at all of these in more detail later on.

Cisgender/cis The opposite to transgender, cisgender (or cis for short) means 'on the same side of' and is used to refer to people whose gender is the same as their assigned sex, which applies to most of society (99.5 per cent of society based on the 2021 UK census). The 'cis' prefix is used in more context than just gender. Cisalpine. Cisplatin. Cisgender. Some people don't like the term 'cis' or 'cisgender' because they feel it's a new label being placed on them. In reality, it's just an adjective, a describing word, and an easier way of saying 'not transgender'. It also avoids othering trans people when it's contextually relevant to distinguish between transgender and cisgender people. So instead of saying 'trans men and men', we'd say 'trans men and cis men', as both fall under the umbrella of 'men'.

Gender conformity/nonconformity Terms used to describe how much a person presents and behaves in a way typically expected for the gender they're living as. For example, a cis man who presents femininely would be seen as gender-nonconforming, and a cis man who presents masculinely would be seen as gender-conforming. Trans people will commonly have been gender-nonconforming before they came out as trans, but it's not a requirement, and many trans people are gender-nonconforming to their true gender after they transition. Gender conformity/nonconformity is related to gender expression and doesn't impact gender identity.

Gender dysphoria A discomfort people can feel when there is a mismatch between their gender identity and assigned birth sex. It can manifest in different ways for different people and be worse over some things compared to others. For example, one trans man may have a lot of dysphoria over his chest, and another may have minimal chest dysphoria but a lot of dysphoria over his voice. Although it's described as a discomfort, it's more than feeling very full after a Christmas dinner! It's intense and relentless, and I can best describe it as a desperation to not be in my own skin. Certain situations can be a trigger of gender dysphoria being felt more intensely, and this can be vastly different from person to person. We'll go through some of the more common triggers through this book.

Gender euphoria The opposite of gender dysphoria. This is a positive feeling, including comfort, when thinking about your true gender.

Gender expression How anybody presents themselves to others (and themselves!) in terms of masculinity, femininity and androgyny. Gender expression is separate to gender identity – in fact they're very different. Gender expression isn't about who you *are* but how you *express*. It's largely based on stereotypes of what girls and boys typically like, so people who wear make-up and heels would be seen to express femininely, and people sporting short hair would be seen as expressing masculinely. People don't need to express in ways that would typically be expected for their gender identity.

Gender identity The feeling of our inner sense of self, and the gender we *know* we are. If assigned birth sex is the genitals, and gender expression refers to what you put on your body, I guess gender identity could be seen as referring to the gender you know you are in your head. This can be different to assigned birth sex, and this difference is what makes trans people, well, trans!

Gender Recognition Act 2004 An Act of Parliament in the UK that allows trans people to legally change their sex on their birth certificate by applying for a Gender Recognition Certificate (GRC).

Hormone Replacement Therapy (HRT) The formal name for the process of trans people taking either testosterone (for trans masculine people) or oestrogen (for trans feminine people). Not every trans person will take hormones, but many will. More on this later!

Intersex Refers to people who are born with sex characteristics, including genitals and/or chromosomes, that do not fit the typical pattern of binary sexes.

LGBT+ The acronym used to refer to people who are not cisgender and straight. They can be cisgender and not straight, or transgender and straight, but not cisgender *and* straight. Specifically, LGBT+ stands for lesbian, gay, bisexual and transgender (and the + is for other identities including queer, intersex, pansexual, Two-Spirit and asexual).

Non-binary Not relating to or involving just two things. In the context of gender, it's used to refer to people who do not have a gender that falls within the binary of either being a man or a woman. Some non-binary people describe their identity as falling somewhere in between 'man' and 'woman', while others describe their identity as falling completely outside of the two terms. Non-binary people are typically seen as falling under the umbrella of 'transgender' as their gender is different to their assigned sex, but not all non-binary people identify with the term 'transgender'.

Outing When a trans person's transness is shared without their consent/behind their back. This can create uncomfortable situations for trans people, and even put them in danger depending on who they are outed to. Outing can happen to any LGBT+ person whose identity is shared without their consent.

Pronouns In the context of gender, Pronouns are the words you'd use to refer to someone: for example, 'he/him/his', 'she/her/hers', 'they/them/their'. There are others too, though these are the most common. There are also non-gendered pronouns, such as 'I' and 'you'. Pronouns seem to be a pretty contentious subject that transphobes have a real issue with, and some institutions have gone so far as to say they're banning pronouns – not sure how that would work! But at the end of the day, everyone uses pronouns, and it's super easy to respect someone's pronouns. Using the wrong pronouns for someone deliberately is often referred to as **misgendering** (bonus little definition for you).

Sexual orientation Someone's identity in terms of which gender (or genders) they're attracted to. There are different labels used to describe sexual orientations, including:

- *Heterosexual, or straight* - attraction to those of the opposite gender

- *Homosexual, or gay/lesbian* - attraction to those of the same gender

- *Bisexual, or bi* - attraction to two or more genders

- *Pansexual, or pan* - attraction to people based on factors other than gender

- *Asexual, or ace* - little to no sexual attraction or desire to have sex (but this doesn't mean they never have sex)

- *Aromantic, or aro* - little to no desire to form romantic relationships while maintaining a desire for sex. People can be both asexual and aromantic.

Stealth When a person is living as their true gender but doesn't disclose that they're trans to people in their lives, such as friends and colleagues, they're known as being 'stealth'.

TERF/gender-critical Trans-exclusionary radical feminist (TERF) was a term originally used to separate radical feminists who are not anti-trans from those who are. The term has since become less favourable as it's clear that TERFs aren't actually feminists, but try to hide their transphobia under the guise of feminism. They don't stand up for the rights and equality of all women, and many only speak up when it's about excluding trans women further rather than on actual issues of women's equality, even those that relate to cis women. That's why terms such as 'gender-critical transphobes' and simply 'transphobes' are being used more, as it doesn't include the word 'feminist' under false pretence.

Top surgery Surgeries performed on the chest. It's most commonly used to refer to a bilateral mastectomy undergone by some trans masculine people (and there are two types of procedures for this which we'll get into later on) and breast augmentation undergone by trans feminine people. Not all trans people feel a need to have top surgery though, and these medical procedures can also be undertaken by cis people.

Transitioning The process that transgender people go through to live, and to better reflect the characteristics typically associated with their gender, as opposed to their assigned birth sex. This can involve social (or non-medical) transitioning steps, and medical steps.

Trans femme/trans masc Terms that cover trans people who fall outside the binary of man or woman, as well as binary trans men and women. Trans masc is a broad term to refer to trans AFAB people (trans men and non-binary trans masc people), and trans femme is a broad term to refer to trans AMAB people (trans women and non-binary trans femme people).

Transgender/trans An adjective used to refer to people whose gender identity is different to their assigned birth sex (which accounts for about 0.5 per cent of the population according to the 2021 UK census). 'Trans' is a prefix that means 'on the other side of', and just like 'cis', it's used in more contexts that just gender. Translucent. Transportation. Transgender.

Transness This isn't a real word, but I find that it fits so many contexts and I end up using it quite a lot! When I say 'transness', I'm referring to the state of being a trans person – which is much more of a mouthful, so I'm sure we can all agree that 'transness' is both easy and cute.

Transphobia An aversion to, dislike or prejudice against transgender people that's solely based on them being trans.

Triggers A wide range of things (actions, contexts, words, smells, etc.) that can evoke strong feelings or memories. Trans people often experience triggers of gender dysphoria. For example, using certain terms to describe the anatomy of a trans person, or misgendering them.

There might be some words that you've seen or heard of that aren't great to use. Most of these are considered bad because they're grammatically incorrect, outdated or have been adopted by people who don't respect the communities they were originally created for, and so can now cause harm. Here are a few relating to the trans community that are generally best avoided:

~~Transgenderism~~   ~~The transgenders~~   ~~Sex change~~

~~When you were a girl/When you were a boy~~

~~Tr**ny~~   ~~Trap~~   ~~Hermaphrodite~~

~~'Choosing to' or 'deciding to' transition~~   ~~THE surgery~~

~~Changed sexes~~

That's about all the definitions I can think of, but do remember that language is always evolving. You might find this challenging, or maybe even think it's unnecessary, but the reality is that language has always evolved so we can come up with better words to reflect our society and culture. Words like 'nerd' have different (and more positive!) meanings now than they used to, and could you *imagine* a world without the words 'Wi-Fi' and 'meme'?!

> Words are powerful, and it takes minimal effort to use them respectfully.

Now go forth: you're officially prepared to read this book!

1

SO YOU THINK YOU MIGHT BE TRANS?

'I was cycling one day and the people behind
me said, "Follow that boy on the girly bike!"
And instead of saying I was actually a girl,
I shouted, "It's not a girly bike!"'

Felix, 19, trans man

Maybe you're feeling scared, worried, shocked, relieved, confused, happy – all of the above? Whatever you're feeling right now, that's perfectly normal. Coming across the term 'trans', thinking you might be trans or realising you're trans are all big moments that can come with a lot of different emotions. **None of them are wrong.** In this chapter we'll be going through the self-discovery process, from questioning to figuring things out.

For me, there was a bunch of relief mixed with a sprinkling – okay, a great big dollop – of fear, and just this sense of *Why didn't I figure this all out earlier?!* Not that there is such a thing as 'too late' or 'too early'. Your journey is your journey, no matter how long it takes, but it just made so much sense to me when I did find the words to describe myself. It helped explain how I'd been feeling for as long as I can remember, and it seemed so obvious when I finally had the language to express it.

The Early Years

Ever since I can remember, I thought I was just one of the boys. For the most part I rejected anything that would associate me with being a girl – not that gender conformity is the be-all and end-all, but because my child brain made a connection between doing and wearing stereotypically feminine things and being seen as a girl, which was something I very much wanted to avoid.

I also simply enjoyed things that were stereotypically more masculine. I liked playing football with the other boys; I wanted my hair short; I only chose clothes from the boys' section for much of my pre-teen childhood. I remember one particular haircut when I was about eight years old. When it was finished I turned to my mum and asked, 'Do I look like a boy now?' Her answer was something along the lines of, 'If that's what you want, dear.' Looking back at photos of me from that time, the answer was absolutely yes!

I feel like my childhood is filled with so many little moments like these. Moments that made me think, *Well, duh! How did I not realise I was trans a lot sooner?!* Like the time I cried about having to wear a dress to my grandparents' wedding anniversary and ended up wearing what was essentially a long glorified T-shirt, or the time in school when we had to place stickers on a map of the playground to show where we spent most of lunch break playing. The teacher gave me a pink sticker, of course, and mine ended up being the only pink dot in a sea of blue. Typically, kids try to fit in with others of the same gender group; they want to be accepted into these groups, and I stuck out like a sore thumb.

Adhering to more stereotypically masculine things is always what's made me feel more comfortable, and it's what I've been drawn to from a young age. Of course, this isn't to say that all kids who are non-conforming are destined to be trans. Gender expression is not the same as gender identity. For me, it's something that goes beyond toy preferences, haircuts, clothing and activities. It was connected to an internal sense of *This is who I am*. I truly believed that I was supposed to have a blue sticker that day at school. I viewed myself as the same as the other boys, and therefore behaved and presented in ways that would lead to me fitting in with them.

WHAT WERE SOME OF YOUR 'I SHOULD HAVE KNOWN I WAS TRANS' MOMENTS FROM CHILDHOOD?

'Thinking my penis would grow/appear once I became a teenager.'

Milo, 24, trans man

'One of my peers commented that they wished their chest was as big as mine, but I felt awful and wished I could get rid of it.'

Luan, 20, trans man

'I asked my parents to shave my head right before I started primary school.'

Arden, 29, trans masc/trans guy

'If my friends were playing house, I would choose to be the kid. Not the son or the daughter, but just the kid whose gender wasn't specified.'

Eli, 23, agender

'When I was playing a woman in high-school theatre and was sad when I had to come out of costume.'

Charlie, 28, woman (trans woman/intersex)

'Age five, my mum tried to put me in a dress for a family photo and she had to chase me round the house because I didn't want to wear it.'

Jamie, 20, trans man

'When I was six I couldn't recognise myself in the mirror. What I felt didn't align with what I saw.'

Louis, 24, trans man

'I grew up always wanting to be a mermaid – specifically a mermaid and not a merman, though. I would be adamant that I didn't want to be a merman and start crying if somebody suggested it.'

Amity, 18, trans woman

'I was ecstatic at being "misgendered" at a restaurant by the waiter, while my mother was horrified.'

River, 21, trans man

'The time I went into a boys' toilet in primary school thinking that was where I should go.'

Jaiden, 22, trans masc agender

While it was my experience, and is quite common for trans people to reflect on, this isn't a definite feeling or expression that all trans people experience. Being non-conforming isn't a must-have on the checklist of 'Am I really trans?'

WERE YOU CONFORMING TO YOUR ASSIGNED SEX IN CHILDHOOD, AND DO YOU FEEL THAT IMPACTED YOU REALISING YOU WERE TRANS?

'I used to do a lot of contact sports (mostly rugby). I stopped playing when I came out due to societal pressures of femininity. I have now returned to them as I genuinely enjoy playing. There are a million ways to be a woman and some of us like contact sports!'

Charlie, 28, woman (trans woman/intersex)

'My parents weren't super big on enforcing gender roles, and I liked a mixture of "boy things" and "girl things" so I really didn't question anything until I was older, in college (20 or 21 years old). Not feeling out of place as a child contradicted a lot of trans stories I'd heard and for a while had me convinced I couldn't be trans.'

Jess, 25, non-binary

'Although I did hang out mostly with boys growing up, I still tried to present feminine as much as possible. And when I became a teenager, I started presenting hyper-femme to fit in. So when I came out as an adult most people who knew me were shocked.'

Melvin, 27, trans man

There's no definitive flowchart or formula that you (or any parent or guardian) can follow to double-check you've got it right. To be honest, the checklist of being trans essentially starts and ends with: 'Is your gender different to your assigned birth sex?' There's a bit more to it than that to be diagnosed with gender dysphoria, but asking yourself this basic question is a good start. There's also no need to know the answer straight away. Don't be afraid to explore those feelings, and know that it's not always a linear journey to understanding who you are.

I came out multiple times throughout my life, and so do many people! It's okay if it takes you a while to figure things out, it's okay if you come out in steps, it's okay if you come out as an identity and then realise it's not right for you. It's your process and whenever or however you figure yourself out is okay.

As I became a young teen, my internal feelings of what I wanted to do, what I wanted to wear, what made me comfortable and happy and who I was all crumbled under peer pressure. I was bullied, basically. And it SUCKED. Mostly I was bullied for being too masculine and being 'different'. I remember going to school one day with a new blue bomber-style jacket on and a particular group of girls teased me about how I looked like a boy and shouldn't be wearing a jacket like that. It was relentless and eventually I felt too self-conscious to wear the jacket to school anymore. I begged my mum for a different coat because I was fed up with the comments.

Now when I tell you I ended up getting the UGLIEST coat you've ever seen, I got the ugliest coat you've *ever* seen: brown faux suede, knee-length, with cream-coloured fake fur around the cuffs, collar and in vertical and horizontal lines across the coat, separating it into squares. Tyra Banks would sob. But the first day I wore it to school, these girls literally applauded me for 'finally looking like a girl'.

It made me feel so uncomfortable, but also relieved that maybe they'd leave me alone. They didn't, of course. Next, it was scrutinising the fact that I wore trousers, then it was because I was friends with boys, then it was just generally the way I acted. The moral of the story is: you shouldn't change for others, as bullies will always find a reason to pick on someone. Knowing that didn't help, though. I felt like there was always something wrong with me.

Feeling this pressure to be more stereotypically feminine, and constantly being told I was a girl and so I should act like XYZ, made this big bubble of discomfort grow. I could never put my finger on why I felt that way, or why I struggled to fit in so much. For a long time I put it down to confusion over my sexuality. Cue a long, winding, convoluted journey of self-discovery and over-analysing my crushes.

Delightful.

It all started when I came out as bisexual to a small group of friends at the age of 14. A couple of years later I came out as a lesbian during my first year of sixth-form college. Referring to myself as a lesbian never felt right, though, because I knew that wasn't who I was. But if I was attracted to women, and everyone was telling me I was a woman, then why did it feel so wrong? It was because I'm not a woman – ta-da! No amount of forcing myself, being told by others or trying to pretend that's who I was could change that. And this monumental discovery came about when I was nearing the end of my first year at sixth-form college.

It was a perfectly ordinary evening. Nothing unusual or ground-breaking about it, and I had no idea I was about to make a discovery that would literally change my life. That sounds like it could be the start of a horror story! I might have been scared for a time, but don't worry, this is definitely a positive chain of events.

How It Happened

I was flicking through TV channels, as you do, and I ended up on a documentary called *The Boy Who Was Born a Girl* on Channel 4. The title intrigued me – the one and only 'yay' I will give to a sensationalised trans headline.

It was about a young trans guy who was transitioning while in secondary school. He was talking about how he'd felt in childhood, his journey of self-discovery, the bullying he'd received at school and then his experiences during his initial few months on testosterone.

I started watching it, not thinking much about it, and as the show went on and the trans guy described his feelings and his identity, I suddenly had this moment of: *HOLY. SUGAR. PLUMS ... Could I be trans? What does this mean? Surely not. I can't be. But wait. I've felt like this as long as I can remember. No. Couldn't be. Could this be it? Really? THERE'S A THING CALLED TRANSITIONING? What does this all mean? Oh. My. God.*

Help.

That was the general gist of my internal monologue while watching the documentary. I've always described it as a bit of a lightbulb moment, albeit a flickering lightbulb before fully turning on. But I'd finally been given the language to describe something I hadn't been able to talk about before, not even to myself because I'd had no idea what it meant. Now I did, and holy wow was that ... scary? A relief? Joyful? I wasn't sure to be honest.

Having a whole range of emotions is perfectly normal.

There's nothing wrong with those emotions being 'negative'. This is often a huge moment for people, and it can be very overwhelming and confusing.

What were your first feelings the moment you realised you were trans?

Relieved   Happy   Didn't feel as alone   Scared

Curious   Unsure of what to do   Anxious   Joy

Freedom   'Hope Mum and Dad will still love me'

Overwhelmed   Confused   Euphoric

'Will I ever find love?'   Conflicted   Sad

Everything made sense   Terrified   In denial

Desperate for it not to be true   Excited

A lightbulb sparking on

'Shit, wait, this explains a lot!'   Clarity

Weight off my shoulders   A 'eureka' moment

Surprised   Hopeful   Hesitant   Nervous

'Oh, wow, people like me exist!'   Absolute panic

Comforted   Worried   Trepidation

Feeling like I needed to hide it

'Aw, shit, okay'   Ashamed

<u>Like I was myself.</u>

There's No Right or Wrong Way

There's no right or wrong way to find out you're trans. It used to be very common for trans people to only discover the word 'transgender' and realise their gender identity through meeting other trans people, or coming across sensationalist media pieces about the latest 'sex change scandal'. Historically, transgender people were rarely spoken about in Western culture, and there's not been a general level of education or discussion on the topic within society.

Even in 2011, when I was near the start of my journey, being transgender (or any LGBT+ identity, for that matter) wasn't formally discussed in schools; and more widely than school settings, being trans was generally not as known in the same way being LGB was.

Social media has changed how we communicate and share news, and one outcome of this is more discussion and increased awareness of trans people. Social media removed the gatekeeping of whose stories could be told, allowing anybody to have a platform, spread education and help others feel represented. Trans people are able to share their lives and who they are, and humanise the trans experience in a way that's not been done before.

The less brilliant impact of social media has meant that the hate and stigma that has always been around can now be shared, and in many ways amplified, with algorithms and newsfeeds creating echo chambers and rabbit holes that encourage people to click on scary titles that cause cultural divides rooted in fear.

But despite this, it's definitely a positive that the word 'transgender' has become more well known, because for the people who are struggling to find the words to describe how they are - like I was - it's literally life-changing, and you're not in control of when that moment happens. If you don't know something exists, then of course it makes sense that you wouldn't know who you are until learning about it.

As information around being trans has become more widespread and accessible, more people have had the opportunity to figure out who they are, and thus there's been a recent increase in referrals to gender clinics. This does not mean that more awareness is *making* people trans. There's no social influence or trend going on when it comes to people being trans. It's to do with people actually having the knowledge to be able to understand their own feelings.

☆ **Top Tip:** *Do what feels right for you; only you know how you feel.*

WHAT WAS THE MOMENT YOU FIGURED OUT YOU WERE TRANS?

'I think I was 14 and said to some friends something along the lines of, "Everybody would rather be a boy," and then I realised that's not actually the case.'

Felix, 19, trans man

'I was 26. I'd suspected for a couple of months. I was putting on some make-up and dressing for a job interview when I realised that all that felt wrong.'

Dante, 29, trans man

'I was 34 when I had a near-death experience that made me reassess my life – or rather, reminded me that I actually wanted to live in the first place. I was reading an interview with a trans man online for some reason and everything they said resonated with me. Something clicked and that was it.'

Anon., 37, non-binary/trans masc

'I was 23. I wanted to try on some of my partner's clothes and the acceptance and euphoria I felt just built from there.'

Eve, 26, trans woman

'I was 15 years old when I was doing an exercise where we had to draw how we saw ourselves in the future. I just couldn't draw myself grown up as a woman ... I drew someone very androgynous. And I knew that what I really wanted to be was a man.'

Jonathan, 30, trans man

There's also no right or wrong *time* to find out you're trans. It's so important to emphasise that **it's never too late**, and it's also never too early. We don't question cisgender people on whether they are too young or too old to know who they are, or nit-pick at things about their behaviour and/or presentation to question if they're really cisgender or not. So why does this happen to trans people? It can be hard to trust yourself when it feels like the world doesn't trust you.

There also doesn't need to be a breadcrumb trail of clues leading you to figuring out who you are. Some people figure it out before learning what transgender means, and other people will know deep down for many years before putting two and two together.

Over the years I've received countless messages from people unsure if they're 'really trans' because of X, Y or Z. Some people think that they've found out too late in life, and therefore if they were *really* trans they'd have known earlier. Others think that because they didn't have any 'signs' or feelings in childhood, then surely they can't actually be trans. Both are incorrect. This is your life, your identity and your journey. You'll probably get bored of me saying this:

no single identity journey is the same.

The Science of Being Trans

This feels like a good place to quickly skim over trans scientific research. I say skim not because I want to rush over it (I did a PhD: I love a good bit of science), but because, as trans people, we don't need to rely on peer-reviewed papers to know who we are. However, it can sometimes be reassuring to know you're not alone or 'weird' for feeling how you feel.

Many papers support that socially and medically

transitioning reduces dysphoria and increases the wellbeing of trans people.[1] Some papers strongly support a biological basis of gender identity[2] and suggest that being trans is a result of hormone exposures when you're developing in the womb.[3] Some scientific research has found similarities in the brain structures of trans women and cis women.[4] Not to toot my own horn, but my own research supports this pattern too, where trans men's arousal patterns were more similar to what you'd see from cis men rather than cis women.[5] That's all pretty cool if you ask me! But again, scientific papers aren't the golden nugget you need to fully understand who you are (sorry). It's more of an internal research process that you have to carry out for that one.

Self-Exploration Is Key

Given my absolute lack of knowledge around being transgender, that one documentary might have sparked my self-discovery journey, but it wasn't the end of it. I

1 'The Role of Gender Affirmation in Psychological Well-Being Among Transgender Women' (2016), Glynn et al., *Psychology of Sexual Orientation and Gender Diversity*; 'Effects of Testosterone Treatment and Chest Reconstruction Surgery on Mental Health and Sexuality in Female-to-Male Transgender People' (2014), Davis and St. Amand, *International Journal of Sexual Health*
2 'Evidence Supporting the Biologic Nature of Gender Identity' (2015), Saraswat, Weinand and Safer, *Endocrine Practice*
3 'Sexual Differentiation of the Human Brain: Relation to Gender Identity, Sexual Orientation and Neuropsychiatric Disorders' (2011) Bao and Swaab, *Frontiers in Neuroendocrinology*
4 'Male-to-Female Transsexuals Have Female Neuron Numbers in a Limbic Nucleus' (2000), Kruijver et al., *Journal of Clinical Endocrinology & Metabolism*
5 'Patterns of Genital Sexual Arousal in Transgender Men' (2021), Raines et al., *Association for Psychological Science*

well and truly fell down a very deep, winding rabbit hole of Tumblr (yes, I am a fossil from the Tumblr era) and YouTube. I'd spend entire evenings scrolling back through Tumblr pages to the beginning of time – including one called 'Lesbians Who Look Like Justin Bieber' (it didn't help me on the trans front but it was an amusing side quest). I was looking to not feel so alone.

I had already begun exploring my self-expression a bit before I learnt about being trans. College allowed me to be more open with what I was wearing (there was no school uniform), and this led me to realise that I was still more comfortable presenting in a more stereotypically masculine way, as I had done as a child. I started buying my clothes exclusively from the men's section of clothing stores, and suddenly had way more interest in clothes and what I wore (funny that). But this was also what led to everyone else assuming I was a lesbian – cue further sexuality confusion!

I also gradually cut my hair shorter and shorter. I never went for a big dramatic chop, I was too nervous (more on this in Chapter 6). As my hair got shorter and shorter, it really increased the amount I was referred to as a man, which was something that made me feel confused, mostly (confused because I liked it and didn't understand what that meant for a really long time).

Some people will have started elements of this self-exploration before realising they're trans, like I did. Self-exploration might be something that helps someone realise they are trans, while others will begin their exploration after realising they're trans. Regardless of the timeline, my rabbit hole of self-exploration, both online and exploring my own presentation, was invaluable in helping me fully figure things out. I experimented with different clothes, hairstyles, etc., until I found things that made me feel as comfortable as I could be. Self-exploration is so important to do if you're unsure about what you want and what makes you comfortable. Don't be afraid to try different things while discovering your own identity.

Very important note: you do not have to change your self-expression at all. You don't need to wear anything or have a hairstyle that is more typical for a certain gender identity. For example, if you think you might be a transgender man, you do not need to express yourself in a more masculine way. Your gender identity and expression are separate things, which do overlap for a lot of people, but they don't have to.

You do you.

☆ **Top Tip:** *Talk to someone about how you're feeling. If you have someone you personally know and trust, great. If not, that person can be a medical professional. You don't have to be sure you're trans or absolutely know you want to medically transition in order to be referred to a gender clinic or speak to a specialist. They're there to help you with your feelings around your gender identity, whether you're sure or not. If it turns out that transitioning is right for you, then you're already on the right path to getting the support you need. If not, it's great that you could get the support to help you learn that.*

What Does It Feel Like?

One of the most common questions that I get from people who aren't trans, or who perhaps think they might be, is: 'What does it actually feel like to be trans?' I wish there was an easy answer but it's one of those things that, unless you experience it yourself, is quite difficult to convey exactly how it feels. For me, coming across that documentary and realising that being trans was 'a thing' felt like coming across a puzzle piece that finally made the image of me make sense. I knew there was a picture there, but I didn't know what it was until I came across the word 'transgender'. It sounds so cheesy, I know. Blame 17-year-old dramatic teenage me.

Another analogy that I read somewhere that resonated with me (and is thankfully less cheesy than a puzzle piece!) involves shoes. It was a small throwaway line, and I can't even remember where I found it, but it stuck with me and became a metaphor that I built upon quite a lot. It's the idea that, for your whole life, you've been wearing a pair of shoes. They function, they're shoes. They protect your feet, you can walk in them – great. But they just don't feel right. There's a constant underlying discomfort that you can't quite put your finger on, and you're not even sure if it's anything to do with your feet. But then, one day, somebody randomly and very innocently points out that your shoes are the wrong way round. Suddenly the discomfort makes so much sense. You can pinpoint where it's coming from, you know what's caused it, and you know there's something you can do to change it. Now to embark on the journey of switching the shoes around!

HOW WOULD YOU DESCRIBE THE FEELING OF BEING TRANS?

'It's like wearing a mask. You don't understand why everyone only sees that mask and why they can't see what's going on behind it. The alleviation when you can finally take the mask off and be the real you ... that's incredible.'

Leander, 18, trans man

'Peace. I am comfortable in my skin. Being myself is like taking a rock out of your shoe, the constant pain has gone.'

Charlie, 28, woman (trans woman/intersex)

'Learning something for the first time that afterwards you think should've been obvious or common sense.'

Ian, 21, trans man

However you find out, whenever you find out, however long it takes you to find out – this is your journey. Be true to yourself, and what makes you happy and comfortable.

💜 **For the Allies:** *Maybe you're feeling scared, worried, shocked, relieved, confused, happy – all of the above? That's all normal too. At the stage when someone in your life is questioning their identity, you may not be (probably won't be) involved in how they're feeling.*

It may simply be that you've noticed a few things that have led you to wonder if someone in your life might be trans. Maybe they've dropped a few hints, or maybe you've walked in on them watching something on their computer and them hurriedly shutting the lid (could also be porn, but you never know).

Whatever it might be that has raised your suspicions, at this stage the best thing you can do is allow that person in your life the space and time they need for exploration, while indirectly showing that you would support them, such as expressing support for a trans character in a TV show. I'm so grateful that when I was a kid my parents just let me wear what I wanted and express myself in the way I was comfortable, and they continued having this attitude throughout my life. Being allowed to express yourself, even before you fully know yourself, is invaluable, and I think that's one of the best things you can do to support a trans person in your life. Let them be themselves, but give them the freedom and space to fully explore what that might be.

Two of the most supportive people in my life have been my parents. I asked my mum to very honestly share how she felt when she was realising I was trans, and what advice she'd give to allies who might just be realising someone in their life is trans too.

CHRISTINE, JAMIE'S MUM:

When Jamie told me he was trans, my overriding feeling was concern. Not for me or my husband, but for Jamie and what his life would be like. I wasn't thinking about babies – that felt far too distant – but would people talk to him? There's a lot of negativity in the discussions you hear about trans people that worried me. Would he be ostracised by society? Would he have any friends? My second thought was: Why do you need to do this, can't you just live life the way you are?

Jamie had mentioned to me that he was having feelings around his gender and wanted to talk about it, and he educated me very well as we watched videos online of other people. Other parents' reactions, other trans people, people who had friends and partners. Learning about it, understanding it and listening to your child is really important. And if your child doesn't have the capacity to lead you through that, my advice would be to be proactive. Listen to what your child is saying and trust them. You know your child, and I knew Jamie. I knew that him sharing this with me was unlikely to be on a whim.

Now I don't have any feelings of concern whatsoever. I don't think of Jamie in any other way than my son, our son. Okay, he had another name at one point and that was tricky to change because it was so hardwired. I never felt like I lost a child, I really never felt like I lost anything. He's just the same. I can go shopping with him now the same way I did 20 years ago when he'd drag me round the shops! Jamie was always Jamie.

2

BUILDING THE REAL YOU

'I found my will to live again.'

Benjamin, 27, trans man

Now we're going to be chatting about those next steps when you've kind of figured yourself out, or you *have* figured yourself out but you're still processing what that means to you. There's a moment in between realising you're trans and being ready to share that publicly, and that's what this chapter is all about. Self-acceptance, self-exploration in terms of pronouns, names, likes and dislikes. You've discovered this big thing about yourself, and that's really freeing, but what does that actually translate to in day-to-day life? Maybe it's a lot, maybe it's nothing. The steps we're going to discuss can be explored in any order that's right for you, and you don't need to go through each and every step outlined here. Remember: this journey is yours.

After that initial *Oh my goodness* moment of thinking you might be trans, and the subsequent figuring out, whatever form that may take ...

What in the hell do you do next?!

Just like a shiny new Lego set, it's time to open the box and tip out the pieces to build your newly found self. Except you can bet the instruction manual is a little more complex – and in some cases completely non-existent.

I feel like when I figured out I was trans, my next main step was working out what that meant for me and my future. It was like taking myself apart brick by brick, without really knowing how to start rebuilding myself into who I truly was.

You Deserve to Accept Yourself

First things first: self-acceptance. There's always so much said about surrounding yourself with accepting people, and what to do if others don't accept you. That's all important too, but there's very little focus on just how important accepting *yourself* can be. People often forget that

*the first person that you need to
come out to is yourself*

and just because it's you, it doesn't mean you'll take it well!

My personal journey of self-acceptance centred around realising **there is nothing wrong with being transgender**, and therefore there's nothing wrong with me for being trans. The media narrative around the time I was figuring things out had definitely instilled in me a negative view of what it meant to be trans. It was all sensationalised articles, in which trans people were rarely shown as anything more than a punchline.

But being trans is just another way of being human, and there's nothing wrong with it. Seeing other trans people living their lives and talking about their journeys, online in particular – beyond a hammy article – really helped me with this.

This journey of self-acceptance can be super quick for some, and longer for others. Regardless of how long it takes, the most important thing to keep in mind is that you deserve to accept yourself.

WAS THERE ANYTHING IN PARTICULAR THAT HELPED YOU ACCEPT YOURSELF AS TRANS?

'Me, within myself, I don't think I had a problem accepting this side of myself. Much like with my sexuality, I thought, *Yeah, kinda saw that coming.* The problems came later when I realised that the world isn't kind to people like me.'

R, 30, trans man/non-binary

'One of the main things was the euphoria of presenting as a woman and people around me using my new name and pronouns.'

Eve, 26, trans woman

'Youth groups and community resources helped me come to terms with who I am. They helped me experiment with pronouns and names and be much happier with my identity.'

Amity, 18, trans woman

'I had so many great trans-positive friends who helped create a safe space for me to explore my identity. I will forever be grateful.'

Matt, 26, trans femme enby

'Having other trans people in my life to talk to, especially ones who were older and were happy, gave me hope that I could grow up to be like them.'

Sanjay, 30, transgender man

'Seeing famous trans people live their best lives helped a lot. I needed to know that I was not alone, that it would be possible for me to be happy, and that there were people who cared.'

Leander, 18, trans man

Self-acceptance: check! What I tackled next were my pronouns, and a new name. You know, just a couple of tiny things, no big deal ... (Total sarcasm.)

The World of Pronouns

Gendered pronouns are such an integral part of everyday life because it's very difficult to avoid using them. They seem like such a small thing, but they can make a big difference. Similar to the way seawater wears away at a cliff, hearing the wrong pronoun used about you can have such an astoundingly negative impact on your wellbeing. Imagine being subtly told a hundred times throughout the day that you're not what you say you are. It hurts. On the other hand, the use of a correct pronoun that you resonate with can be incredibly affirming and the highlight of your day, even if it's from a total stranger who you'll never see again (sometimes that makes it better!).

Pronouns were very easy for me. I'd figured out I was trans, and for me that meant figuring out I could live as the man I know I am. He/him/his were the pronouns that felt right for me. I decided on these pronouns before I told anyone I was trans.

It isn't that simple for everybody, though. There are many different options when it comes to pronouns, the most common being she/her/hers, he/him/his and they/them/theirs. Typically, trans men would want to be referred to as 'he/him', trans women as 'she/her' and non-binary people as 'they/them'.

Some people will also feel more comfortable using a combination of pronouns, such as she/they or he/they, and others aren't fussed about what pronouns are used at all.

It's also not uncommon for people to adjust their pronouns over time and after further self-discovery. Maybe you start off using gender-neutral pronouns like they/them, but later realise that she/her is who you are, or vice versa. You're never wrong to change.

'I originally came out for a little bit using they/them pronouns, since I was too scared of what people would say if I used he/him. I later used he/him pronouns when I felt more comfortable, and the people around me made it very safe for me.'

Taryn, 18, trans man

If you're unsure what pronouns to use and you're not out to people in real life, a great place to try them out is in online spaces. Forums, blogs, online support groups, friends, social media profiles – you get the gist. You can include pronouns in your bio in a lot of places now, and joining online support groups is a great way to introduce yourself with pronouns you're road-testing. Shaaba and I see this quite a lot when we livestream gaming, and honestly, it makes us so happy! Baby trans people will introduce themselves in the chat and the rest of us help take their possible new name or pronoun for a test run.

☆ **Top Tip:** *Outwardly open online safe spaces are a great opportunity to explore your identity in a place you feel welcome in. See how it makes you feel when others refer to you with a certain gender, name or pronoun, or you introduce yourself as that. It can really help solidify your internal feelings.*

But 'Them' Doesn't Make Sense?

They/them/their gender-neutral pronouns have become a point of particular fury from transphobes who often claim that 'they' can't be used in a singular context. If a transphobe has said that to you, they're incorrect (and this sentence just proves it). Everyone uses 'they' and 'them' in a singular way on a frequent basis, often without even noticing! Another example I hear you ask? 'Somebody left their pizza behind' – a travesty, but an example of a singular usage of they/them/their. There are instances of 'they' being used as a singular pronoun in literature as early as the fourteenth century. It's not a fad, and it's not unusual.

That's it for pronouns here, but there's a little more in Chapter 6 if you're interested. Now, let's talk about a more exciting type of noun – your name!

Hello, My Name Is ...

For most people, a name is an integral part of their identity and who they are. It's what comes to mind when people think about us or talk about us, or even to us. It's what's shouted when we're in trouble (that one's less great). In short, names are important, and trans people get the (somewhat) unique opportunity to pick our own name – just try to resist the urge to say, 'Thanks, I picked it myself!' when someone compliments you: the novelty wears off after a while!

When choosing my name, I felt like I had a lot of responsibility and was almost overwhelmed by the amount of choice I had. When you name a baby, you're choosing a name that you feel suits a crying blob that hasn't developed hobbies or a personality yet, and the name becomes who they are as they get older. But when you're choosing your own name, it feels like your selection has to suit you automatically, and that can be STRESSFUL. What if I made the wrong choice? What if I didn't like the new name I picked over time? It's good to be reminded that just like with pronouns, you're allowed to change your new name if it doesn't feel like a good fit.

I didn't decide on Jamie until after I'd come out to quite a few people. I actually came out saying that I wanted people to use he/him pronouns, but I had no idea about my name yet.

I struggled with picking a new name, and I changed my mind about it a couple times: Jamie was not my first. *Dun, dun, dun!* Shock horror!

I still felt hesitant over changing it, though, like I had to be loyal to a name. It's normal to feel this way, but you really don't owe your 'draft' names anything. The first name I tried was one my parents would have called me had I been assigned male at birth. I asked them, turns out they'd had one, and it felt like the most natural option. I trialled it on sites like Tumblr, and with a therapist I'd found who, despite specialising in 'gender identity', was

49

relatively unhelpful to me personally. The most useful thing that came out of those sessions was realising that my name choice just didn't suit me. Even though I hadn't been using it for very long, or with many people, I still felt this awkwardness and almost embarrassment that I'd gotten it wrong. But I'm here to remind you that it's totally fine and nothing to feel bad or embarrassed about!

I had a list of other names I liked, and my top choice was James, but 'James Raines' doesn't have the best ring to it! I also wanted to keep the same initials: J.A.R. (I'm not sure why but I liked the fact that my initials spelt 'jar', ha-ha.) So Jamie felt like the next best option to try. Without skipping ahead too much, Shaaba was the first person to use it. The same day I came out to her, she asked me what she should call me now. I told her what was top of my list, I liked how it felt, and everyone said it suited me. Job done!

First names are important and all, but don't discount a middle name too (if you want one, of course – it's not a necessity). It's still part of your name and will appear on official documents, so it's important to consider. For me, there were only ever two options for a middle name: Andrew or Anthony. The previous middle name also started with 'An–', and has sentimental value to my mum, so I wanted to stick with the same vibe to honour the history the name has for my family. Anthony was my favourite from the offset, so after some experimenting, I landed on:

Jamie Anthony Raines.

☆ **Top Tip:** *It might sound strange but using the same methods that parents use to name babies can be really* *useful. From baby-naming books to apps where you can see name options in full and swipe right or left on names you love or hate can work really well. Involving your parents or loved ones in this process can also help you and your closest allies feel more supported during this fundamental change too. We'll talk more about this in Chapter 6.*

WHAT INSPIRED YOU TO CHOOSE YOUR NAME?

'My name is Noah and I chose my name because it reflects who I am as a person, and because the meaning behind the name is opposite to that of my deadname.'

Noah, 23, trans man

'My name is Alice, and that was inspired by the rock singer Alice Cooper.'

Alice, 21, trans man

'My name is Taryn and my mum inspired me to choose the name: it's what I would have been called if I'd been born a boy.'

Taryn, 18, trans man

'It's simply a shortened version of my birthname. It's comfy.'

Matt, 26, trans femme enby

'I looked at what I wanted my name to mean on an Indian baby name site and picked based on that.'

Sanjay, 30, transgender man

As you can see, everyone's process will differ slightly, or maybe a lot in some cases. **It doesn't matter how many trial names you have** or how long it takes you to pick a name.

It's also not essential: some people choose not to change their name when they transition. If you're comfortable and happy with your birthname and feel that it suits you, then there is no necessity to change. Most trans people change their name due to dysphoria caused by having a name that's associated with the wrong gender, as that can cause misgendering to occur, especially early on in a transition journey. But not everyone has dysphoria or discomfort over the same things, and if your name is something that works for you and that you want to keep, then go for it!

A lot of people think Jamie was my birthname because it's fairly gender neutral, particularly in the States. The neutrality of it wasn't important to me at all, as it's actually a more masculine name in the UK, which I guess shows just how varied names can be. Ultimately it's a name that I like and that works for me, regardless of other people's perceptions of it.

💜 **For the Allies:** *Asking a trans person what their birthname was is never a cool thing to do. It can cause significant discomfort for most trans people, and it's also not important for us to know. Similarly, if you happen to know a trans person's birthname, you shouldn't share it with others who don't know, even when asked directly. Asking a trans person about their birthname doesn't help you understand or support* *them any better, it's just to satisfy your curiosity, and it's never the role of trans people to satisfy your curiosity. – Shaaba*

What You Wear

As a trans person, I've spent a lot of time feeling pressured to wear certain things. As a pre-teen I felt I had to wear more feminine clothes to fit in and avoid bullying, and when I first came out I thought I needed to reject anything remotely feminine. But that's not the case. You're totally free to explore what you want to wear, regardless of what section of the store the clothes come from. Have your hair in whatever length or style you want, and experiment with different ones to see which suits you best (yes, I've just decided that you wear hair). Enjoy the exploration and lean into or away from those stereotypes of gender expression as much as you like.

What You Like

As well as being free to explore what you want to wear, you can also rediscover and explore what you like to do. Your interests and hobbies don't need to be dictated by the expectations of others. People are often boxed into certain hobbies depending on gender. It was a given in my school that basketball and rugby were for boys and netball and hockey were for girls (who even decided this?!). Even away from certain sports, there's so much heavy stereotyping going on when it comes to hobbies. Sewing, gaming, woodwork, scrapbooking, fishing, journaling ... I'm sure we could all think of how a lot of people would gender these hobbies, but don't let these stereotypes hold you back. Take some time to figure out what you truly like, not what you've been told you should like because of your assigned birth sex or your true gender.

❤ **For the Allies:** *This stage of self-discovery may not even be something you notice very much. Maybe that certain someone has had a recent haircut, a shift in their wardrobe, or they might be consuming far more YouTube than average (hello, rabbit-hole-of-not-feeling-alone). Maybe you don't notice anything at all. Many trans people often go through this self-exploration phase alone. It can be a confusing time, with a lack of certainty in how to proceed.*

As a not-so-subtle segue into the next chapter – this can mean that when/if they come out to you as transgender, it might come as a shock. It could be that someone has just come out to you and you're feeling pretty surprised by that news, but this likely won't be a new discovery for that person, and it's important to remember that a lot of thought has likely gone into this already.

Intersectionality

As well as the very individual factors of what we like and dislike, recognising group characteristics and experiences can also help frame who we are as people. Gender, race, sexual orientation, religion, social class and more – these are all factors that form our identities and experiences, and different combinations of these factors can mean our journeys are significantly different to other people's. It's also important to realise that different combinations of these factors can also lead to varying levels of privilege and oppression, a consideration that surrounds intersectionality.

Trans people are no exception to intersectionality, where being trans is just one part of who you are and what impacts your life. For example, I'm transgender, but I'm also a man, a white person, an able-bodied person and am from a middle-class background. While these aspects of my identity may not seem to have anything to do with my transness, they're all interlinked. The fact that I'm white and able-bodied makes me more likely to be middle class. The fact that I'm white and a man means I face less discrimination after transitioning. The fact that I'm from a middle-class background is likely impacted by the fact that I'm white and, in many ways, has made my transitioning journey easier. Everyone has a different combination of intersectional identities that influence how they experience the world, as well as how they're perceived and treated by others.

Shivani Dave is a 27-year-old journalist, broadcaster and physicist. They produce *The Log Books*, an LGBT+

history podcast, and have shared some of their experiences around their intersectional identity as a South Asian non-binary person. Look out for Shiv again in Chapter 10, where they explore non-binary identities in a little more depth.

SHIVANI DAVE

I am a second-generation immigrant. My family are originally Indian, and I grew up in a Hindu household. Growing up, a lot of my friends were South Asian/ Indian too, but when I first came out as bisexual, I ended up losing a lot of them. We all went to different universities, and it was hard to see them still hanging out and no longer inviting me.

A few years after I came out, there was a study published by the BBC Asian Network [linked in the Further Reading section] about how British Asian attitudes are typically more socially conservative than the rest of the UK. It helped me understand the lack of LGBT+ acceptance in the community I'm from, and empowered me to be more visible and vocal about my identity.

My extended family have had mixed responses, from not accepting any part of my LGBT+ identity, to trying to encourage me to get conversion therapy, to being okay with the 'bi stuff' but not the 'trans stuff', to being fine with it – but only if I don't shout about it. I've ended up distancing myself further from all these kinds of relatives, but have a brilliant immediate family who love and celebrate all parts of me.

It's a minefield I have to navigate within the LGBT+ community too. Not all spaces, events or people are anti-racist, so it can be a challenge to feel welcome sometimes. Being in east London, there are more than enough options for me where I can feel comfortable and embrace my heritage, as well as my sexuality and identity. It wasn't easy to find these spaces, but they are there.

Now What?

So you've done a little bit of exploring here, changed up your expression there, maybe tried a new pronoun or two in several places, you've picked out a new name. But now what?

Maybe it's time to think about sharing how you've been feeling with others. Taking that self-exploration and self-discovery and being able to live openly as who you've discovered you are. No worries if you're not ready for what's in the next chapter (spoiler: it's the how-to-come-out chat). You can hang around in this section for as long as you need to. There's no rush.

3

THE WHO, HOW, WHERE AND WHEN OF COMING OUT

'I had kept it to myself for so long. All the signs
were there and I just had to tell people. I felt
like I would explode if I left it any longer!'

Theo, 27, trans masc/non-binary

Welcome to the coming-out chapter – this one's a BIG ONE. Not to scare you at all, though. Pfft, coming out? Piece of cake ... Nope, sorry, I can't do it (no one ever said being LGBT+ was easy!). Coming out is a big step. It can be exciting, a relief, but often, it can be scary. This is the moment you start letting other people into your world and your identity, and that's a pretty big deal.

Congratulations on reaching this point, whether you're just starting to think about the process of coming out, if you're feeling ready and just need a final pep talk before the big moment – you're doing great! While it would be wonderful if coming out wasn't such a big deal (and that would be the case in an ideal world), unfortunately it still is, so tips and advice are still important.

We're going to get into the specifics of the who, how, where and when of coming out. The A–Z of telling people you're trans, if you like. The bit that makes most people go

AHHHHH.

Don't worry if that sounds like an overwhelming number of things to consider, it will all come together (hopefully) throughout this chapter. Saying that, please bear in mind that this information is meant as guidance. An 'if you need/ want it' resource. You absolutely don't have to think it through this deeply – coming out can absolutely be more spontaneous! This is just some info in case you want to plan it a little, or have no idea where to even start ... or both.

The overall piece of advice I'd give is that the possibilities are endless. It's all about what makes you feel most comfortable, safe and able to talk as openly as possible.

The Who

I'm starting off with 'the who'. Not the band, but literally who to come out to. **This can often be the biggest decision and can influence the how, where and when.** I think the who is also crucial, as knowing that you have even just one person's support can make a world of difference in the early days of your transition, and can really help with coming out to others. Even if they aren't involved when you come out to others, knowing you have that support behind you can be a huge reassurance.

Have a think about if there's anyone in particular you trust, and feel would likely be supportive of you. Is there anyone who has shown general support for the trans community, or a different trans person in their life, that you feel you could come out to?

For me, this person was my mum. I've always had a good relationship with my mum, and she'd accepted me with no questions asked when I'd come out as a lesbian about a year before. I think she'd already suspected something because it didn't seem to surprise her. More on my personal story later, though.

The first person you tell does not need to be a parent. It doesn't even need to be another family member, or even a friend you know in real life. Just make sure you trust whoever you tell with the information you're giving them. It could be that you come out to someone who is part of a support group you've been going to, or a teacher at your school. Maybe even a colleague at work, or an anonymous support helpline.

WHO WAS THE FIRST PERSON YOU CAME OUT TO, AND WHY THEM?

'A teacher at school. I just felt safe with him, and it would have felt too real if I'd told anybody else. He was a more neutral person to tell first.'

Felix, 19, trans man

'I came out to someone on a pen-pal app first as it felt like a safe environment that was separate from my day-to-day life. Therefore, saying the words didn't have an immediate impact on my life.'

Luan, 20, trans man

'My husband. I didn't even think about it. I was reading an article, something clicked, I realised and I yelled, "I'm an idiot! Of course I'm trans!"'

Anon., 37, non-binary/trans masc

'The friend who'd come out to me and who'd helped me understand my own identity. I came out to them almost by accident the moment I realised I was trans.'

Asher, 23, AFAB non-binary

'I came out to my mum and my sister because they pressured me into saying why I looked like a boy.'

Leonardo, 20, trans man

Sometimes the first people who know you're trans may not have known you before you realised. You might have met someone at a support group that you've only ever attended as your true self. I've met lots of people at Pride events, for example, who were there as themselves for the first time and were literally coming out to strangers before anyone else, and making new friends who already accepted them.

☆ **Top Tip:** *If you know who you want to come out to but you're struggling to predict how they'll react, it might help to try and gauge their general opinion of trans people. You could try bringing up someone who's trans in conversation, putting on a TV show with a trans character, or speaking to them about a trans-related* *news story and seeing how they react. A positive reaction isn't necessarily a guarantee that they'll accept you, but it can be a good indication that they're at least not super transphobic.*

Try to make sure, as best you can, that whoever you tell first is someone you trust and feel safe around.

The How

Now you know who you want to come out to, the next step to think about is *how* you want to come out.

People come out in all sorts of ways, from the super creatives who cover their houses in rainbow sticky notes, to the basic-bitch method of: 'Hey, I'm trans.' (Absolutely no offense intended here: this was 99 per cent of how I came out. There's nothing wrong with a classic!)

The 'how' of coming out is not just in what you say, but how you say it. You can tell people face-to-face or in an email or text (which may feel impersonal to some, but this is your coming out and you should do it how you want), a phone call, classic snail-mail letter, a highly trained carrier pigeon, sky writing (I wrote this as a joke, but high-key love the idea) or perhaps a message in a bottle strapped to the fin of a great white shark.

Choose whichever way makes you feel most comfortable.

Maybe not the shark one, though – sounds slightly dangerous and unpredictable.

It might be that you choose different 'hows' for coming out to different people. If you're going down the en-masse route, maybe a social media post? I've seen this work well for others who've put something on their Facebook wall, or have made an Instagram post explaining they're trans, so please use X name and pronouns from now on.

I personally went down the route of telling those closest to me in person, and then just creating a new social media profile (I only had Facebook at the time) and adding the people I'd told, and new people I met, as I went along.

It might be that other people can help you, or 'be your how', by being present when you tell someone else, or by telling others on your behalf if you've asked them to. I asked my mum to tell my dad for me. I wasn't scared that he'd react badly, but we didn't have super deep chats despite being close, and I didn't know how to address the topic with him. I regret not telling him myself, though, especially as he was very supportive straight away, so it wouldn't be my top piece of advice. Hindsight is a wonderful thing, and it would have been nice to have told him in my own words and been there to answer any questions he might have had. I also feel that symbolically it would have shown him how important he is to me, but honestly you have to do what's right for you in that moment. As long as it's with your explicit permission, it's totally fine to ask other people to share your coming out. I gave my parents permission to tell family friends and more distant relatives whenever it came up, and it avoided me having to have *that* conversation a bajillion times. But if it's to close family or friends, you might just want to consider how the recipient of that news might feel about not hearing it directly from you.

When it came to my friends, I told them all in a group. Well, all except Shaaba ... that was the only mildly creative coming-out moment I had, but more on my story later ... First let's get to some more advice for you.

On to the where!

The Where

This might seem like an odd one. *Like, what the heck do you mean, WHERE do I come out? As if there aren't already a million and one other things to think about, I now have to choose a particular coordinate?* But hear me out,

the environment in which you come out can make a big difference.

The where can range from sitting around the dinner table, to being on a roller coaster just as it enters a loop-the-loop (I can't promise I'll stop with the unrealistically funny examples).

Despite my silly suggestions, the 'where' has a more serious angle as well. The term 'home advantage' isn't just related to football, and you might find that being at home, in an environment where you feel most comfortable and in control, helps. Alternatively, you might find that being in a more public setting like a cafe or going for a dog walk in the park suits you better. Consider if there's a risk of a strong reaction, even in a public setting, but being around others might discourage heated arguments or raised voices, and provide a more civil opportunity to walk away for a breather if necessary. No one should have to consider something like this when coming out, but it's so important to make sure you're in a safe situation.

It might be that you decide not being in the same room as other people is the best 'place' to come out. That's where the letters and emails could come in, or FaceTime or phone calls for a more social touch (or pigeons and sharks for the more ludicrous ... Sorry, I'll stop now).

The When

This one's kind of the BIGGEST of the big ones of coming out. When on earth do you do it? The only right answer is: whenever you're ready. It can be after you've felt ready for a while, but

never feel pressured to come out before you're ready to.

You've probably had a lot more time to think about your transness than the person you're telling has, so timing your coming out can be important, as it's likely going to be pretty big news for them and might even take them by surprise. It's your journey at the end of the day, but it is a good idea to consider whether the conditions you plan will get the best response, and whether you're likely to have someone's full attention (rollercoasters are probably a no-no), especially if they're going through a stressful time. Other than that, time is your oyster.

☆ **Top Tip:** *You might want to consider timing your coming out with a particular date, especially if you're feeling a bit overwhelmed with choice. For example, National Coming Out Day is 11 October every year; many people plan to come out on this day due to the significance and confidence it can provide.*

The 'when' might also be dictated by the 'who'. I certainly felt ready to tell some people much earlier than others. Family first, for example. Close friends before acquaintances. And sometimes when I had planned to tell groups, it didn't quite work out that way. Even the best laid plans don't work out sometimes, and that's okay.

Sometimes, the 'when' of coming out can have a big build-up and then just not happen. Maybe the words just don't want to come out after all. Maybe plans fall through, or it starts raining, or there's a traffic jam, and now the mood isn't quite right anymore. It might take you a couple of tries before you feel completely ready to hit 'send'. All of this is A-okay.

HOW DID YOU KNOW YOU WERE READY TO COME OUT, AND WHEN DID YOU DO IT?

'There wasn't a particular lightbulb moment or event that led to it. It just slowly built up with me thinking back to all the previous times I had questioned my gender identity, and built until I felt I needed to come out.'

Eve, 26, trans woman

'I'm not sure if I ever felt ready. I kept setting myself deadlines, like my birthday, or National Coming Out Day. One day I decided I might regret coming out, but I'd definitely regret never coming out, so I might as well do it. I don't regret it!'

Jamie, 20, trans man

'I knew I would come out in the summer holiday between changing schools, but it took me a few weeks to find the courage. I ultimately came out the night before we went on our family holiday, which made for a very emotionally intense evening!'

Daniel, 19, trans man

'I had been questioning my gender for a while since coming out as bisexual, and one day just decided to post who I truly was on social media, because I was tired of holding myself back. I made a cute post with a selfie, and was well supported in return.'

Matt, 26, trans femme enby

Sorry, What? This Is All Too Much.

The who, the how, the where, the when. It's a lot. In truth, you're almost certainly going to have to consider each one of these multiple times as you come out to different people, in different ways, at different times.

Try not to worry. You'll likely not consciously think through each stage as separately or rigidly as I've outlined them here. Each part will influence another, and it will naturally become the process by which you tell different people that you're trans.

Coming out will also be an ongoing process.

I used to think it was a one-time thing, but nope. There will be a bunch of people that you specifically want to tell at the beginning, and then in dribs and drabs, but to be honest, coming out is almost certainly something you'll find yourself doing long into your transitioning. There will be new people in your life you might want to tell, or people you knew before that you've since reconnected with. There will also likely be new people in your life you might not necessarily want to tell, but will still have to. For example, if you get a new job before changing certain legal documents, or you start seeing a new medical professional.

Remember, though, coming out is your process and should always be your choice. Go at your own pace, plan it (or don't plan it!) as much as you want and always prioritise your safety.

My Personal Experience

I want to share the who, how, where and when of how some of the most important coming-out moments came together for me.

My mum was first in mind. She was the person I found it easiest to talk to, and she'd accepted me when I'd come out as a lesbian straight away (pun fully intended). She's a very open-minded person, and I'd always gone to her for advice on all sorts of different things. I told her earlier than I probably felt completely ready to, about three months after watching that documentary, but I also felt I needed someone to talk to about what was going on inside my head. I was feeling pretty lonely and figured I could talk to her about how I was feeling, rather than waiting until I was ready to fully come out.

We were talking in my room one evening when I said I was having some ... feelings over my gender. I asked if we could talk about it. I showed her some of the videos I'd watched about other trans guys talking about how they felt, starting testosterone, and even Q&As with their own parents (those ones really helped my mum understand how to better support me). Yes – I even showed her some Tumblr blogs. I'd planned to gradually introduce her to what being trans was before fully telling her I thought this was me. She figured out that I wanted to pursue medically transitioning before I told her – I was probably way more obvious than I thought I was being!

The next person to find out was my dad, but as I mentioned, I regret it wasn't from me. I just didn't know how to say it, but he was so accepting. My mum told me that the first thing my dad said was: 'That's okay, he can have my spare razor.' Turns out I wouldn't need it for about four years, ha-ha, but it was a relief to hear such a typical Dad response! I definitely have a closer relationship with him since I've transitioned.

My dog, Benji, also took it quite well! My mum has more distant family that she told over the years whenever it was relevant/necessary to. I don't see my extended family much at all, but I recently went to visit some of them in Glasgow, 11 years since I came out. They were so lovely and supportive in a very genuine way, and I feel very lucky to have family like that in my life. They're also well into their seventies, and had no issues accepting me – so age is definitely not an excuse!

I'd built up a small friendship group throughout my first year at college, and I wanted to tell them all in one go, just rip off that Band Aid. It was the summer holidays, I was 17, and I'd loosely planned to finish my first year as *deadname*, and start my second year as Jamie. We were all set to meet in the local park one day. It was public, so I knew I could leave if I felt uncomfortable. I also hadn't told my friends I had something important to say, so I knew if I didn't feel ready, I could just not say it that day. Everyone showed up that day except for Shaaba, my best friend at the time, now my wife. Typical!

I told the others that day, pretty much by saying, 'Hello, there's something I've been wanting to tell you. I'm trans, could you please use he/him pronouns for me from now on, new name pending, thank you very much.' They all kind of shrugged and said, 'Okay.' At worst I don't think all of them understood what I meant by 'I'm trans', but they all were respectful and started switching over pronouns straight away.

The last close person in my life I came out to was, of course, Shaaba. It was difficult for us to see each other outside of college because she was living in a very strict household and wasn't allowed to socialise much. But she came over to my garden shed one day during the holidays, which sounds stranger than it was. It's more of a very old, slightly damp, summer house where I'd play drums. There was an armchair and beanbags, and she could tell I was nervous. And I was *super* nervous about telling Shaaba. She was my best friend, and I was scared of losing her the most. I stumbled over my words a lot until eventually I asked her if she knew what the term 'LGBT' meant. She said yes, very definitively from what I can recall. 'Well,' I said,

'I'm the T in LGBT.'

I got a totally blank look back. Utter silence. I was sweating for a second thinking she didn't accept me or something. We stared at each other for a moment until she admitted she knew of the acronym, but didn't know what the T meant. I still think this was a pretty smooth way to come out – if she'd had any idea what I was talking about! It was a relief to know the silent stare wasn't a lack of acceptance though. I explained it all, what transgender meant – that it's who I am – and she was honestly *amazing*. I felt like her perception of me instantly changed in a positive way, and she was seeing me for me. Shaaba's the only person who literally never messed up my pronouns right from the start. She helped me test the name Jamie that day too.

The final big coming-out step was to my college. I knew teachers would have to know, and my name change needed to be registered. I was shitting myself about that one. I asked Shaaba to come with me to a meeting I'd arranged with my senior tutor (I needed her to actually walk me right up to the door, otherwise I might have run away). I explained what was going on to a very nice teacher (thank you, Mr Kelly). He was understanding, supportive and explained clearly what the college could do to support me. They could change my name on registers, email and my student ID, and let my new teachers know what was happening. They asked me if I wanted to move form groups and bring a friend with me (Shaaba, obviously), and changed my class groups so I could minimise any awkwardness and reduce how many people I'd need to come out to personally. It worked great because my college was large enough that I sort of slipped under the radar.

💜 **For the Allies:** *How my parents, friends and college handled my coming out was invaluable to me. I'm so lucky to have had that support, and I hope my account of my personal experience gives some useful tips on how to provide allyship from a range of positions.*

I started my second college year as Jamie, and I'm very grateful for the experience I had coming out. I lost a few friends and acquaintances who just stopped talking to me (news travels quick in these settings!). I heard the whispers, I saw the staring; it was uncomfortable, but easy to ignore. It got a bit worse when Shaaba and I started dating around six months later. One person liked to tease Shaaba, constantly asking her if she now 'batted for both teams'. He generally made lots of people feel uncomfortable, to be honest. But I had my close friends I could hang out with, and I ignored everyone else.

I definitely did face a lack of acceptance and transphobia – from more distant sources, like teachers who didn't even know my name, to much heavier sources, like Shaaba's family in particular, but more on that in the next chapter.

💜 **For the Allies:** *Coming out is one of the biggest and scariest steps someone will take. The best thing you can do as an ally is let them do it in their own time, and be there for them when they tell you. Even if you don't understand, you can still be accepting. Ask how you can be supportive, do your best with new names and pronouns, and remind your trans loved one that they're so worthy and deserving of love. It's okay to have concerns about the stigma that they'll face, and it's okay to voice those concerns, but also voice how much you're rooting for their success! It's also okay to feel shocked, and to need time to process. It's even okay to not understand. If this is the case, please take the time to listen to trans voices, try to understand better and let the initial wave of shock pass before reacting in a* *way that may feel hurtful. Finally, know that whoever is coming out to you is still the same person they were before. Your support will create the best environment for them to flourish as themselves and make their lives so much easier.* **Not supporting someone won't change who they are, it will just make their life harder.** – Shaaba

What If You're 'Outed'?

You should be, and always deserve to be, in control of your coming out.

In control of who knows. In control of when and how they're told. But unfortunately that's not always possible. Sometimes people will decide for you and tell others. It's never okay for someone else to take your coming out into their own hands.

I've personally experienced multiple incidents of being outed to others, and it can lead to some very uncomfortable moments. Two that stand out to me both happened at university, over a year after I came out as trans. I didn't have any real following online at that point.

Shaaba and I lived in a flat and had a spare room, and one of Shaaba's friends was looking for a place to live. She was dating one of our old friends who'd been there when I'd first come out at college, but she herself didn't know I was trans – she'd only ever known me as Jamie. I was debating whether or not I wanted to tell her. At this point I'd been out for a few years, I was over two years on testosterone, and I'd had top surgery. Part of me felt it was information she didn't need to know, and I quite liked having people in my life that I could just be Jamie to, without the history. But at the same time, I was contemplating telling her, because if she was living with us, I didn't want her to find out by overhearing something.

While I was weighing this up, her boyfriend's mum outed me to her. I found out when she texted Shaaba to ask if it was true. Fortunately, she was accepting towards me, but I was upset that the decision had been taken away from me. What had been said? Was it said in a calm way, or as gossip? Did she know my birthname now? It was pretty frustrating.

The second time was at a trans student meet-up at university – the last place you'd expect an outing to occur, right? It was the first meet-up of its kind and I'd gone along because a friend from my course had come out as trans, and they'd invited me. At the time, I was very private about being trans, and this trans friend was the only new friend from my course that I had told. Before going to the meeting, I'd made sure it was closed, and only other trans people would be there. Can you see where this is going?

Partway through, another member of the LGBT society walked in. An out cis gay man, who knew me, but not that I was trans. He popped his head in to check everything was going okay (instantly not making it a safe and closed space), looked round the room, and left. A couple of days later, Shaaba got a text from a friend: 'Is Jamie trans?' I was shocked. She was shocked. And I was mad. They had told this mutual friend that I'd been at the meet-up. I don't know if he'd told anyone else, but telling this one person was bad enough. I never went back to another trans meet-up during my time at university.

💜 **For the Allies:** *Outing someone is never okay, whether it's coming from a good place or not. Finding out or knowing that someone is transgender (or any other LGBT+ identity) is not gossip to share with others. It can create situations that are anywhere from awkward to hostile to dangerous for the person being outed. What might seem like juicy news among friends could have huge repercussions for the trans person being spoken about, so don't out people, and if you feel safe to, discourage others from doing so if you see it happening.*

HAVE YOU EVER BEEN OUTED? IF SO, WHAT WAS THE OUTCOME?

'When I started a new job, all of my new co-workers were told there would be a trans person starting (me). I never got to gauge the situation before they all knew. I am pretty open about my identity, but it was disappointing that it wasn't up to me to decide who at my new job would know.'

Asher, 23, AFAB non-binary

'Someone outed me to an extended family member, who then texted me sharing their (unsupportive) thoughts on me being trans. I was angry, and baffled at how they thought it was any of their business.'

Ian, 21, trans man

'A family member once outed me to another family member, not maliciously. The person I was outed to was supportive, so it wasn't harmful, but I still felt there was a significant breach of trust as it was done without my consent. It felt somewhat violating.'

Eve, 26, trans woman

'I have, and I felt extremely violated and embarrassed as I hadn't accepted myself yet. The outcome was ridicule, and I actually went back in the closet and hyper-feminised myself for years. Now I look at it as a reason to stand up for myself and younger me.'

River, 21, trans man

'A year after realising I was trans, I confided in my doctor. She then outed me to my mom, who was in the waiting room. My mom was a bit taken aback and confused – the waiting room and my home had never been so silent. A few weeks later, I came out to my mom myself to reclaim the power the doctor had taken.'

Rowen, 18, trans man/masc

Whatever stage you're at in your (inevitably many) coming-out journeys, you've got this! Come out in a way that feels right for you, and remember there is always support out there. You're not alone.

4

WHAT ABOUT ACCEPTANCE?

'My mum at first was not comfortable with my identity, but has since come to the realisation that she'd rather have a son than no child at all. I think that was a hard thing for her to reconcile. When she saw that she wasn't losing me because I was trans, but could lose me if my mental health deteriorated, that helped our relationship get back on track.'

Graysen, 29, trans man

Coming out is a BIG step, with a capital B, I ... and G. Maybe I've mentioned that before? The aftermath can be big too. Lots of big stuff going on. Sometimes acceptance is instant, sometimes it can be tentative and take time, and sometimes it never comes. Whatever the outcome, know you're incredibly awesome for coming out, and you're absolutely deserving of living your best authentic life.

We all hope for – and deserve – acceptance and support when coming out. This chapter covers those trickier moments when those you come out to struggle with accepting you. We're going to chat about how to deal with the lack of acceptance, safety tips and additional places to find support (remember, support is always out there, it just might take longer to find).

Why Would Someone Not Accept?

I've been lucky to find overwhelming acceptance from a lot of the people in my life. Having a public platform brings a lot of hate, but offline, there was only one major source of non-acceptance, and that was Shaaba's family. Some of them were great, but some of them were not so great (to put it politely). Before sharing my experiences from the past, you should know that the most important members of the unaccepting family are now accepting. Eleven years after coming out, Shaaba's mum helped us plan our wedding. I love her, she's my family too now. We both think it's important to show that even people who seem the most unaccepting can completely change their view. Time can be a great healer – not always, but sometimes.

As you already know, Shaaba and I were friends before I came out as trans, and naturally during this time I'd met her family. I'd been over for dinners and parties, and they knew we were good friends. This made it impossible for Shaaba not to tell them when I came out. She didn't want to disrespect me by using the wrong name and pronouns, and equally couldn't pretend that we just didn't talk anymore.

Shaaba accurately predicted they wouldn't accept me, and would try to stop us from being friends. The reasons were multi-layered and complex, and it's more

Shaaba's story to share, but the arguments given to me over the next few years were religion, culture, family reputation and race. 'Being LGBT+ is a sin,' Shaaba was told. 'It's not what we do, just imagine what the family would say.' Shaaba had to abide by a strict 'no friends who are boys' policy, which was used as the main reason we couldn't be friends, yet at the same time, they refused to use the correct name and pronouns for me, so didn't really see me as a man. I realised they had no idea what being trans meant beyond the 'sex change' headlines in the news, and simply didn't want Shaaba in the company of someone like that.

There are many reasons people use, to not accept trans people, either generally as a community, or someone specific in their lives. It's important to remember that people are not born bigoted. These are learnt responses to a way of being that people haven't had the opportunity to learn about, or have been taught to be afraid of, or have been given misleading information about (often it's a combination).

> Lack of understanding, fear and misinformation. These are almost always the reasons why people might not be accepting, but they're rarely the reasons people give.

Nobody stands there and says, 'Sorry, I don't accept you because I don't know enough,' or, 'It's because I've been misinformed about your experiences.' They rarely notice the relationship between why they are non-accepting and the reasons they give, leading to a belief that their viewpoint doesn't come from a bigoted or close-minded place. People don't want to seem like the 'bad guy', and often rely on 'valid' reasons for their lack of acceptance.

These reasons can be displayed in a lot of different ways, most commonly:

- **Religion** Some people use their own interpretation of scriptures and religious teachings to exclude not just trans people, but the wider LGBT+ community (and others too). This isn't to say that all religious people are not accepting, but religion is a frequent reason people give to say they're not allowed to, or can't, accept trans people.

- **Cultural norms** The idea that girls are girls, and do 'girl things', and boys are boys and do 'boy things' is heavily ingrained in many cultures. These strong gendered stereotypes, which some people believe need to be lived by, makes the idea that 'girls' cannot be boys, 'boys' cannot be girls, and everyone has to fit into one of those two boxes. Trans and non-binary people are therefore viewed as something that can't possibly exist within this worldview.

- **Community stigma** Often in groups that have these cultural norms, a breaking of these rules can lead to others treating those rule-breakers differently (from micro-aggressions to more severe shunning), along with anybody who accepts those rule-breakers. This can encourage others who might accept *you* to not be accepting, in fear of the reputation it would give *them*.

- **'Protection of rights'** Increasingly, the protection of women's rights is being used as a reason to deny trans people of equality, particularly when it comes to trans women. This definitely falls under the 'why' of 'misinformation'. Rights are not a pie. Everyone deserves equal rights, and trans people gaining equal rights doesn't take away the rights of anyone else.

I questioned whether it was relevant to outline why people might not be accepting, but ultimately decided it could be helpful to a wide range of different people reading this book. I hope other trans people find it useful to know there are broad reasons for non-acceptance, and that it's rarely personal. Knowing a bit more about where a lack of acceptance comes from might lead to understanding whether anything could help increase acceptance too.

For cis people, including allies, it's important to understand the origins of and variations in transphobia. It's not always people shouting slurs, and it can at times seem harmless. Sometimes, negative opinions about transness might seem 'valid', but typically stem from fear and misinformation, and are ultimately transphobic. These can be quite dangerous factors that fuel a lack of understanding, fear and misinformation.

These are factors that have been around forever, mind you (maybe even the dinosaurs discriminated against each other, who knows), and which help explain discrimination faced by not only trans people, but many marginalised groups within society, including LGBT+ people generally, and people of colour. I don't mean to get super deep on you here, but in a way, it's reassuring to know that trans people aren't being uniquely targeted. It's obviously still problematic and wrong that anyone has to go through discrimination, but it's weirdly comforting to know that the same old tactics are used whenever society has a problem accepting anything other than the status quo. Transphobia is recycled homophobia, and homophobia is recycled racism, and there's still a lot of homophobia and racism around. Don't just take my word for it: psychologists have been studying discrimination for ages, and there's lots of further reading you can dig into if you want.

Factors might include a lack of education, pervasive historical attitudes from older generations, patriarchal thinking and fearmongering with misinformation to fuel culture wars and feed underlying capitalist motives. There are more personal factors to consider, too, like misdirected past trauma or internalised phobias, that are more common than you might think. A whole extra book could be written about all of these things alone (I've listed some great resources in the Further Reading and Resources section), but the important takeaway here is that the trans community isn't to blame.

This stuff is kind of heavy, and I want to give you a very important reminder: although we can list reasons why people might not be accepting, none of these can be used to excuse bullying or discriminatory behaviour. More importantly:

none of the reasons people give for not accepting you invalidate who you are.

What Does Non-Acceptance Look Like?

Time for another episode of *The Shaaba and Jamie Story*, ha-ha. Even though Shaaba's family forbade our friendship, we hung out secretly. To cut a long story short, I told her I liked her that winter after one too many alcopops at my house party in 2011 (typical teenage cliché). We acknowledged we were more than friends but didn't want to label anything, until I sent Shaaba a text wishing her a happy New Year, which her mum found. Their label for us was quite clear: lesbians.

I didn't hear from Shaaba for the rest of the break, but I did get a call from her dad (who'd always been supportive of our friendship) explaining that Shaaba wasn't allowed to communicate with anyone at all. It was the scariest start to a year I've ever had. I remember the moment we first saw each other after that. We stared at each other across a college classroom, both nearly crying. Now I'm crying writing this, oops. I often forget how difficult it was in the beginning. Their non-acceptance of me displayed itself in different waves.

The first was a lot of misgendering, name-calling, slurs and being referred to as a lesbian. This was pretty relentless. When they realised we weren't splitting up, the next wave was that it became a huge taboo for Shaaba to even speak about me. This felt easier than the name-calling, but stranger at the same time, because it wasn't just my gender that was being ignored now but my entire existence.

It was difficult for me, and while I don't want to speak for Shaaba, I do want to acknowledge it was difficult for her too. Ignoring the giant elephant in the room (I'm an elephant now) just made tensions worse over time. Eventually, a boiling point was reached and Shaaba was disowned as a daughter. We've lived together ever since and were grateful to be closer together, despite the circumstances that had made it possible.

It was a bit of a journey to be honest, and the non-acceptance we both experienced ranged from seemingly smaller acts such as name-calling and misgendering, to much more drastic actions, like losing a family and a home.

Non-acceptance can take many different forms. I feel like I'm naming zombies here, ha-ha. Let's call this next one a two-faced lurker. This non-acceptance might look quite innocent, but can cause a lot of harm. I actually find this to be one of the most hurtful. It's when someone seems perfectly chill with all things LGBT+ – even expresses to your face that they're supportive – until it gets too close to home. This could be the friend who accepts that *you're* trans, but boldly tells you they wouldn't accept their own child. The family member who makes an effort to catch up with you at the annual BBQ, but won't attend your wedding and talks crap behind your back.

Then there are the line-dancing zombies: one step forward, two steps back. Acceptance is not always linear, but this non-acceptance zombie really takes the brain (I was going for a 'takes the biscuit' pun, did it work?). It's when you feel like you're making progress, opening up conversations, and moving forward with people who have struggled with acceptance, but just as you see signs

of progress, they regress right back to how they were before, sometimes worse! This back and forth can be incredibly frustrating, but does typically show a progression and an attempt to be accepting. (This inner-conflict non-acceptance can usually be zombie-cured over time!)

💜 **For the Allies:** *Some of the strongest allies to trans loved ones I know used to have line-dancing zombie non-acceptance behaviours. Recognising that you've been unsupportive at times doesn't make you bad. As long as you can use that as an opportunity for growth, it makes you a pretty kick-ass supporter.*

And let's not forget the werewolf zombies (yes, we're doing a supernatural crossover now). These ones seem fine most of the time. They hold your hand and show acceptance every step of the way – until something big happens, like a full moon. That's when they show their true colours and you realise their acceptance of you isn't really acceptance, because it's conditional. People who feel they can give and take away their acceptance of your identity for any reason are being manipulative, even if they don't know it. It might seem like acceptance, but leaving you constantly questioning isn't acceptance at all.

Acceptance should always be unconditional.

It's unlikely that a trans person will go through their journey without experiencing some kind of non-acceptance in one form or another, and it's never a good experience (obviously). But just know that you don't deserve it, and it's not your fault that it's happening. It's also not something you're going to have to deal with forever, and there will be a time when you're surrounded by accepting people who love and respect you for who you are.

Dealing With Non-Acceptance

The good news is: wherever there are non-accepting zombies, there are tools for coping with the horde. Let's have a chat about what tools you should have in your arsenal to best help you when faced with non-acceptance.

WHAT HAS HELPED YOU COPE WITH PEOPLE WHO WERE NON-ACCEPTING?

'I ignore them. If they are not willing to accept my life then I have no interest in continuing to pay attention to them. I am fully aware I am extremely privileged to be so independent.'

Charlie, 28, woman (trans woman/intersex)

'Seeing YouTubers talk about similar experiences and how they coped. Having a supportive friendship group has helped as well.'

Theo, 27, trans masc/non-binary

'I try to remember that it is not really about me – it is about the fear and hatred they have been encouraged to develop by people and organisations who have never met me or put real and good-faith effort into understanding what it is like to be a transgender person.'

Daniel, 19, trans man

'Surrounding myself with positive trans people is important when the relentless barrage of transphobic media is intense. Getting offline and doing something else, such as going to the gym or doing something physically draining like boxing, is vital for my good mental health as a trans person in the UK.'

Jonathan, 30, trans man

Please allow me to share some advice about your arsenal of tools:

Know when to use them. Your safety should always be put first. This sometimes means not saying certain things, or not responding in anger, and knowing when to pick your battles. I'm not saying this to silence you, or saying you're wrong for getting angry. You're entitled to feel anger, and you're perfectly entitled to express that anger. It's also important to recognise that sometimes, acting on that anger isn't always the best thing, and in the worst cases, may even jeopardise your safety. Whether it's a transphobic tweet that you're itching to respond to, or a passive-aggressive remark from a parent, do you need to respond with anger on this occasion? Sometimes the answer is yes, sometimes the answer is no. Sometimes a more thought-out response can encourage discussion rather than defensiveness from the person you're interacting with. Safety is always the main priority.

Sometimes the best tool is to walk away. Not everyone is willing to learn or hear about things they don't understand, and it's not your responsibility to educate every non-accepting person you come across. People may be saying certain things to get a reaction out of you, and being able to ignore them takes the power out of their actions, leaving them shouting into a void. The pressure of wanting to help educate people can be truly exhausting, and it's okay to put yourself first. And I'm not just talking about the internet trolls here – this can happen with people in real life, too. You have every right to walk away from people who are not accepting, be it colleagues, friends, family or whoever that might be.

Focusing on the positive is the best tool. Dealing with negative reactions is difficult, but honestly, the best thing I did in those moments was to focus on the positive. Remind myself of the friends and family I had acceptance from. Remind myself that those negative reactions were coming from a place of ignorance and a fear of the unknown, but they couldn't stop me from being myself, living my life and being proud of who I am.

☆ **Top Tip:** *When you're feeling in a good place, I'd suggest taking the time to create a list somewhere (or in multiple places) of all the good things you have. Scribble down a list of good moments in a notebook. Get your friends to write you supportive messages on little pieces of paper you scrunch up and keep in a jar. Save an album of photos in your phone of good times with the people who absolutely support you, or help you feel joy and pride about your identity. You could even dog-ear the pages of this book that make you feel super happy to celebrate your transness! If ever you feel low, you'll have a great tool of positivity to use. You've got this!*

Sometimes It Takes Time

For three years after Shaaba was disowned, I had no direct communication with her family. Shaaba was barely allowed to see or speak to them, including her younger siblings, in case they were influenced by me to become trans (seriously). Despite this, small steps of progress were being made. Instead of begging Shaaba to break up with me every time they'd speak, her family began to naturally and gradually use my correct name and pronouns. Over this time I attempted to try and start communication with them, to try and make some progress. I bought them small gifts at Christmastime and reached out via email. I wanted to build a bridge and show them I wasn't bad or scary.

The big step forward happened one winter, four years after I'd come out. Shaaba saw her family on Christmas

Day each year, and would pass on a box of chocolates I'd got them. This time, I asked if I could deliver it myself. It took a while to build up to this point. You kind of learn on an individual basis when it's right to give people some time and space, and when it's time to push a little bit. People need to be willing to listen in order for any progress to be made, and pushing when people aren't ready will often result in frustration all round.

I wasn't expecting what happened that afternoon. After going alone to give Shaaba's family a gift, we had a conversation that lasted several hours. It was the first time they'd seen me since before I'd transitioned, and they were so surprised by my appearance. I remember the phrase 'Wow, you'd never have guessed' being used multiple times, and I got a lot of stares of disbelief. They asked me all sorts of questions. How would we have kids? Would I convert? Did I want to marry Shaaba? I gripped a glass of water tightly the whole time! It felt like being on display at a zoo at times. I normally wouldn't have been so polite about it, but I didn't want to cause any friction and realised that this going well could help make things a lot easier for us all. Shaaba's mum in particular was polite, just very direct with her questions. It was clear she was coming from a place of wanting the best thing for her daughter, and being patient was definitely the best approach. I don't think we'd have made much progress if I had been antagonistic or defensive.

☆ **Top Tip:** *You should never feel pressured to answer questions or share information that you're not comfortable with. It's your choice what you share and* *what you don't. Personal information doesn't have to be a prerequisite for acceptance.*

It was at this point that we entered into a long-standing line-dance of zombie non-acceptance with Shaaba's mum. It was another three years of making a bit of progress, and then going back to square one, sometimes for no reason at all. I remember one particularly gruelling email back-and-forth. I'd given up trying to be polite, and stood up for myself, calling out what was wrong with what they were doing.

Part of why there was so much back-and-forth was because there were some outside influencing factors. Speaking with Shaaba's mum now, it's clear to see that things like religion, culture and the influence of other people all acted as barriers to her feeling ready to understand, and ultimately get to a place of acceptance. While I can see that now, it was sometimes difficult to realise that in the moment. Not that influencing factors can be an excuse for discriminatory behaviour, of course, but it serves as a good reminder that somebody's stance on things can come from a place that involves a lot of complexities. Actions towards your identity may not always be a true reflection of someone's thoughts or values, but instead a reflection of the way in which they feel pressured to act.

The line-dancing zombie act stopped in 2018 when I had bottom surgery. We'll talk about the actual surgery in Chapter 8, but spoiler: we didn't tell Shaaba's mum about my surgery until I needed a second emergency procedure, and as fate would have it, she called while Shaaba was having a total breakdown! It became a turning point, though. She brought us food, spoke to the doctors, and told me afterwards that seeing me go through that helped her realise that

being trans was not a choice, but clearly something I needed to do.

Since then, we've had no more line-dancing. It came as a pleasant surprise and a relief that, after all those years, all the negativity, all the stress and hurt, we'd finally reached a point of respect. It took seven years from my coming out to Shaaba's mum reaching a point of true acceptance. I'm not sharing this as some kind of achievement, but to show just how drastically different timings can be when it comes to acceptance. The most important takeaway we learnt from this experience wasn't connected to time, though; it's that

you only truly make progress when people are ready and willing to listen.

I also want to share that while it's great that acceptance eventually happened for us, we didn't wait around for it. We started off doing that. Shaaba in particular did for multiple years, until we realised that it wasn't something we should put our lives on pause for. We initially said we wouldn't marry without Shaaba's family's acceptance, but changed our stance with all the line-dancing. We got engaged without full acceptance from Shaaba's family, because you need to live life for you, and the reality was, it might have never come.

DID PEOPLE'S REACTIONS AND ATTITUDES TO YOUR TRANSITION CHANGE OVER TIME?

'When I came out there was so much conflict, I didn't think I could fix those relationships going forward. But they're getting better every day, and I'm so thankful for that.'

Victor, 20, trans man

'Unfortunately my parents had the hardest time with my coming out. I thought they'd never accept it, but my brother told me they correct themselves when I'm not even around now. We have a good relationship again.'

Melvin, 27, trans man

'My mother often questioned my identity and called me by my deadname which drove us far apart. Now, almost five years later, I know that she did it out of concern for me and was afraid that I would regret my decision. But like me, she's learnt a lot, and today she sees how much better I am. Our relationship is better than ever.'

Benjamin, 26, trans man

'I noticed a lot of people who "accepted" me coming out, yet merely tolerated my existence while not putting in the effort to refer to me correctly, or challenge their own cisnormative ideals. This acted as a filter to help me find who my real friends are.'

Matt, 26, trans femme enby

And Sometimes, It Never Happens

Non-acceptance is difficult, and not something that anybody deserves to experience, but it's also not the be-all and end-all, even if it might feel that way in the moment. I try to think of acceptance as the cherry on top of a very gorgeous cake (the cake being you!). You can survive and thrive and live your life of icing and rainbow sprinkles without the acceptance of people you might have expected – and wanted – it from.

Let me be clear: I'm not trying to trivialise non-acceptance, or pose it as a good thing. It's awful. It's a total betrayal. *And*, at the same time, you deserve to be free from an endless loop of waiting and hoping.

The best piece of advice I've received around unaccepting people is that you don't need to keep them in your life. No matter who they are, or what the relation, if they are a source of toxicity and negativity in your life, and if they do not give you the support you deserve,

you are under no obligation to accommodate negativity.

This is, of course, substantially easier said than done, especially when it comes to those closest in your life, such as family. The good news is, and I can say this with absolute certainty,

there IS support out there. You WILL find acceptance, and you WILL find people who see you for who you are.

They might not be in your life right now. Acceptance can come from all different places - family, friends, colleagues, support groups, online, the moon (dream big). Sometimes it finds you, and sometimes you need to seek it out.

Where did you find acceptance and support?

Friends, friends, friends!

The transgender community

My partner   My school   My siblings

The roller derby community   My dog

Local Pride groups   Trans youth groups

The trans and queer Jewish community

Charities and helplines   Books   Movies

My favourite creators online

☆ **Top Tip:** *If you're struggling, I'd recommend looking into local support groups who meet in person, or even online groups where people share advice and support. In the early days, I found a lot of comfort and advice from Facebook groups specifically for trans masculine* *people, which talked about general support and transition advice, as well as sharing social updates away from being trans. I also see livestreams and Discord servers being a great source of support – I know this, because Shaaba and I have these ourselves! There are so many safe spaces waiting to welcome you with open arms. If you want more info, have a look at the Further Reading and Resources section at the end of this book.*

5

THE BEAST THAT IS DYSPHORIA

'One of the big dysphoria triggers I had in the past was a transphobic cat. A friend said their cat hated guys, and it proceeded to sleep on my lap!'

Rowen, 18, trans man/masc

First and foremost: for trans people reading this chapter, I'm adding an extra trigger warning. I understand several sections of this book might be difficult, but gender dysphoria can be particularly tricky. Please look after yourself and only read on if you think it'll be helpful and not hurtful.

Secondly: in this chapter (and throughout this book), whenever I say 'dysphoria' I'm referring to gender dysphoria specifically, but know that there's more than one type of dysphoria.

Alright, let's crack on.

What Really Is Dysphoria?!

Gender dysphoria is a beast, a great big, massive, HUGE pain the butt, and something that can feel impossible to deal with at times. Sorry, I wish I could be cheerier about it.

In this chapter we're going to have a chat all about what gender dysphoria is; some of the symptoms of it; personal experiences of having gender dysphoria; and ways of coping with it prior to/without medically transitioning. This isn't trying to tell you what you should or shouldn't feel in order to be transgender. Instead, it'll hopefully help you understand what dysphoria is, detect whether you (or someone you know) might be experiencing it, and provide some tips on how to deal with it (or support someone you know experiencing it).

As well as being a ginormous pain in the butt, gender dysphoria can be broadly described as the discomfort caused by being a gender identity that is different to your assigned birth sex.

It can come with a side order of symptoms, like a mismatch between your gender and your primary and/or secondary sex characteristics, or having a strong desire to live, present and be seen as a gender that's different to your assigned birth sex.

Now these are just a few of the symptoms. If you feel you may be experiencing gender dysphoria, I would recommend checking out the complete list, which you can find on websites like the Mayo Clinic and the NHS (full links are in the Further Reading and Resources section).

When it comes to gender dysphoria, everyone is different. Not everyone will experience the same symptoms or feel these symptoms with the same intensity. You don't need to tick off all the items on some imaginary checklist. There can be elements of dysphoria that are internal, and are centred around how you physically sound or look, or more social elements related to how others may perceive you or refer to you.

Gender Dysphoria Pre-Transition

Despite common themes, everyone experiences gender dysphoria differently. About different things, at different intensities - a whole lot of different. Thinking back to a time before hormones and surgery, my top points of dysphoria were my voice, my chest, my body shape and then generally being read as female, or being misgendered. Oh, and hearing my deadname. I swear I could almost physically feel my insides scrunch up and drop out of my butt whenever this happened, especially if it was in front of other people. That was *horrible*.

I remember a teacher at college misgendering me accidentally, and I wanted to run through the classroom wall to get away from everyone. Not the teacher's fault, she was lovely, and it happens sometimes, but my God did it make me feel uncomfortable.

Then there were the times I bumped into people from my past. You know, those people who recognise you, but you've not spoken in years. It was always a choice between coming out to them there and then, knowing that's quite a heavy conversation with someone you'll likely not see again, or just rolling with the conversation and being referred to as my birthname while waiting for the ground to swallow me whole.

For me, the internal dysphoria was what I struggled with the most. You can't escape your own body, and being stuck in a body that was so ... deeply and incredibly uncomfortable felt unbearable at times.

I remember desperately willing my body to start changing in the way I wanted it to, hoping that I would wake up one day and look different. To not have my chest, to not be an hourglass shape, to not have a high-pitched voice. I longed for a beard and a deep voice, and so much more. I wanted to escape my own skin and step into looking a different way – a way that I knew wouldn't cause me this pain and discomfort. It didn't feel like a want, it was a desperate need.

My voice caused me discomfort and also led to me being misgendered the most, so I gradually just stopped speaking in front of others (apart from family and friends), and avoided interacting with strangers as much as I could. I'd say my voice was one of my top points of dysphoria, so it almost felt like I lost it for a while.

The overall feeling of these symptoms of gender dysphoria culminated in feeling trapped. Trapped in a body that made me unhappy, and trapped with people seeing and treating me as someone I wasn't. I was desperate to live my life as who I truly am.

I knew the only option for me was to transition.

WHAT DOES DYSPHORIA FEEL LIKE TO YOU?

'Uncomfortable, like wearing a clown costume and feeling like everybody is staring.'

Felix, 19, trans man

'It feels like a mask that stops people from seeing the real me.'

Eve, 26, trans woman

'So frustrating. Like I'm trapped in a big blob of play-dough and I can't reshape it. It makes me feel held back, like I can't break through the glass to my full potential and where I want to be.'

Jamie, 20, trans man

'It feels like being an alien inside my own body, wanting to hide from the world until I feel like myself.'

Asher, 23, AFAB non-binary

'It feels like something inside of me is being crushed. It torments me to the point I can't look at myself for even a second without spoiling my mood.'

Amity, 18, trans woman

'Like there's something clawing at my skin wanting to break free. Like I'm trapped by skin and flesh and bone, screaming and crying inside my head begging for freedom. Like I'm constantly waiting for permission to breathe, holding in my breath until my lungs burn and turn black and charred.'

Rory, 25, trans masc

Can Anything Help?

Whether or not you're going to pursue medically transitioning, or are at the stage to socially transition, there are a few tips and tricks that might help you deal with gender dysphoria. They might not all be helpful to you, but there will be things (no matter how small they seem) that you'll discover will help with your personal dysphoria. Even if these are things that feel silly, or are ultimately pointless (like working out was for me, haha), give them a go anyway! (Always be safe though, please.)

Binding or padding: I want to make you aware that these things exist: they can change your body shape and help hide areas that might cause you dysphoria. We'll chat about them in much more detail later on in the next chapter, but skip ahead a bit if you're keen to find out more now.

Clothing: This can make a surprising amount of difference, both in terms of how comfortable you feel in yourself and how others perceive you. Put your comfort first and go for clothes that make you feel good. Maybe that's changing your wardrobe over to be more masculine, feminine or androgynous – whatever that might be, give it a try.

☆ **Top Tip:** *Clothes can also be used to help hide or accentuate certain aspects of yourself, which can help with dysphoria. I used to live in baggy hoodies because* *they hid my chest, and darker clothes because they concealed my binder.*

Hair: What you do with your hair can go beyond the affirming moment of cutting it all off or getting your first wig. It can also be about choosing a specific style, or having the freedom to ask for something that seems more typically masculine or feminine.

Exercise: This might sound like a strange one (it definitely isn't for everyone), but working out can also help with how you feel about your body, and change it a little before/without hormones and/or surgery. I'm all about body positivity, there's no size-shaming here. Body dysphoria can be reduced, though, by building muscle and broadening your shoulders for a more masculine look, for example – unless you're like me who struggles to gain any kind of weight. Still, it made me *feel* like I was doing something to reduce my dysphoria.

People: Having as many people as possible in your life (including online) who support you, gender you correctly and will use the right name, can be super helpful in reducing gender dysphoria in social situations. My group started off really small, but it grew as I came out to more people, found trans support groups and made new friends.

WHAT HELPED YOU COPE WITH DYSPHORIA BEFORE YOU WERE ABLE TO START TRANSITIONING?

'Men's soap, deodorant and clothes helped me present as masculine as possible. But mostly, I validated my own identity by using gender-affirming language for myself in my head.'

Leander, 18, trans man

'Singing along to male artists who sing a lot in falsetto. My favourite is Hippo Campus, but since my voice has dropped, I can't sing nearly as high, lol.'

Ian, 21, trans man

'Speaking to other trans people helped so I knew I wasn't the only young trans boy out there struggling with dysphoria.'

Jonathan, 30, trans man

'Going to the gym to build muscle, getting my hair cut short and watching trans YouTubers talk about their experiences dealing with dysphoria.'

Theo, 27, trans masc/non-binary

'Indulging in my hobbies and knowing who I was at the time helped distract me from thinking about how no one else knew who I was at the time.'

Rowen, 18, trans man/masc

💜 **For the Allies:** *You'll never know what gender dysphoria feels like, but you don't need to relate to something to be able to provide help. Going through the stages of transition is the way to ease gender dysphoria, so supporting your trans loved one on their journey is the best way to help. Using the right name and pronouns, going shopping together to help with self-expression, offering support to access trans healthcare (from signing petitions, to helping with gender appointments) will all make the process a little easier for them.* – Shaaba

Dysphoria and Those Around You

Shaaba and I made a skit video about dysphoria once. It was difficult to know how to show what it felt like, and we ended up creating a whole extra character who was like a little devil sitting on your shoulder and making you question everything. Did I have a lot of fun making that video and popping up from the bathtub and from inside the wardrobe with little one-liners? Yes, yes I did. But in real life, no one else can see that silly dysphoria, and that can make it really tricky, particularly when you're experiencing the beast at its worst.

The friends and family around you might not be the only people to not understand dysphoria. For the first couple of years, I didn't even fully realise when I was feeling dysphoric, what made it better or worse, or how to communicate how I was feeling to others. It could be the most bizarre little thing that set it off, and my dysphoric state could either be fleeting, for a minute, or last hours and hours, with no rhyme or reason.

I would retract into myself and be very quiet for a time, or get frustrated and feel hurt and annoyed by the smallest things. It was mostly time that taught me what triggered my dysphoria, and what I could do to help myself. Eventually I learnt how to communicate it to others, and those closest to me learnt that if I was acting irrationally upset, it wasn't anything personal, and we could chat about it when the wave of dysphoria had passed.

☆ **Top Tip:** *Shaaba and I came up with a codeword for me to use when I was feeling dysphoric, as I found it really hard to talk about. I won't share what mine was, but it was something random like 'carrot' or 'chopstick'. It worked great, because if dysphoria hit at a really inconvenient time (like in the bedroom – why, dysphoria? WHY?!), I could just say it and we'd put on a movie no questions asked. Or in public, or during an argument, having that single word would explain why I was acting odd, and give me the space and time to deal with it. Maybe coming up with your own word and having this strategy with a close friend or family member could help you too.*

💜 **For the Allies:** *It can feel really frustrating to not understand what seems like irrational anger or grumpiness when your trans loved one is feeling particularly* *dysphoric – but imagine how they feel themselves! The best thing to do in those moments is to let them know you're there for them and that you'll support them in whatever way they need. You could offer them some time and space alone, and try not get into any arguments in the moment. Feeling dysphoric doesn't leave your trans loved one in the most rational head space to talk things out. – Shaaba*

WHEN IT CAME TO YOUR FRIENDS AND FAMILY SUPPORTING YOU WITH DYSPHORIA, WHAT THINGS REALLY HELPED YOU?

'It helped that people knew what I was going through, and told me things like "You pass" and "Just a little longer to HRT" or just "We see you and love you."'

Benjamin, 27, trans man

'Having queer and genderqueer friends is such a game-changer. Just knowing that I'm not alone and so many people can understand my feelings is really validating.'

R, 30, trans man/non-binary

'Putting effort into getting my name and pronouns right, and understanding that it mattered to me.'

Daniel, 19, trans man

'Affirmation from my supports that I did look quite androgynous.'

Asher, 23, AFAB non-binary

'My older cousin invited me to his stag night and said I could wear a kilt to his wedding.'

Jaiden, 22, trans masc

WHAT THINGS REALLY DIDN'T HELP YOU?

'People saying "Just stop thinking about it" or "It isn't that big of a deal."'

Alice, 21, trans man

'Some people voiced expectations of what they thought I'd do to my appearance. It made me feel like I wasn't doing enough to fit certain expectations, rather than exploring my presentation at a pace I was comfortable with.'

Eve, 26, trans woman

'Getting complimented on things I was dysphoric about or being told no one else notices those things never helped me.'

Eli, 23, agender

'Telling me to just embrace how I looked and try to feel comfortable as I was.'

Asher, 23, AFAB non-binary

'People apologising too much when misgendering me. It put too much attention on the mistake, and not the correction, which felt othering.'

Matt, 26, trans femme enby

Dysphoria and Transitioning

My relationship with dysphoria shifted multiple times throughout the different stages of socially and medically transitioning. The triggers and focal points of what caused my dysphoria evolved. Some got worse (not worse due to transitioning, but because my focus shifted). Many got better, and I'm now at a point where I experience incredibly minimal dysphoria. It's like a grain of sand compared to the entire beach it used to be.

The next few chapters will get into the transition experience in more depth, but I want to cover how transitioning specifically affects dysphoria. Put simply, transitioning for trans people (social and/or medical) is the treatment for gender dysphoria, and has been well evidenced to reduce symptoms successfully.

First things first: socially transitioning. Being totally out and living full-time as myself flung open so many doors for coping with my dysphoria. I think a lot of the time people focus on how much hormones and surgery can tame the beast, but even before these happen (or they might never for some people, as not everyone wants/needs to medically transition), being able to live as yourself can improve things a lot.

I was able to present in a way that made me feel more comfortable. My friends, family and people at college referred to me as a man, and as Jamie (for the most part). I was wearing a chest binder, and I was able to start changing my ID and other documents over to have the correct name and gender marker on. Just seeing things like my Facebook profile having the correct name, and having male pronouns selected, all helped so much.

While it wasn't an easy time, there were so many little moments of joy that I could experience throughout this process. Receiving my name change in the post, having 'Jamie' read out on the register at college, getting a new college ID with an updated photo and name, showing off my new driving licence and bank cards and passport (that was a particularly big one because of the little 'M' gender marker). All these moments helped greatly with the more social elements of dysphoria.

☆ **Top Tip:** *Wait times are long and access to trans healthcare is tricky, so hormones can feel far away. But there are lots of small milestones and checkpoints to reach that can make a big difference. Try writing a list of all the little things within your control that you could change, and set deadlines for them, so you've always got something to aim for on the way to reaching your goal. Keeping yourself busy with studies, work, hobbies and socialising can help too.*

I was incredibly fortunate that misgendering was relatively uncommon for me, but it didn't help so much with the physical side of dysphoria. Yes, I could bind my chest, and I had a little ceremonial binning of my bras (don't ask, it was a whole thing). But my chest was still there at the end of the day when the binder had to come off. I could change my name with the bank, but when calling them up, I would still get misgendered because of my voice. I could buy a new outfit, but I still needed to avoid looking in mirrors when getting ready because I didn't like my body shape underneath.

There was also the lovely added bonus of a shift in my attention. At each stage I focused on what I was able to change myself, and when those things were done, there was joy and relief, but also nothing to distract myself away from the rest of my dysphoria. As I progressed through the social elements, the dysphoria over my appearance and my voice gradually crept back to the forefront of my attention. It then became a game of patience until I could start testosterone, and my patience had to endure *after* I started as well.

Hormones can change a lot of things, but they don't do it overnight.

It took a good six months for hormones to make a real dent in helping with my dysphoria. I was obviously incredibly excited to have started and to see all the little changes begin to happen, but in terms of genuine improvement, it took a while because so does testosterone.

Over time, my voice deepened, my fat started to redistribute which changed my body shape, and I grew body hair. Facial hair came in *much* later for me, but I was content enough sporting a snail trail for a while. I gained some weight and started to actually notice muscle changes – still minimal, but definitely there.

It felt like finally growing into my own skin, and I started to feel like I belonged in my body.

As much as testosterone helped, it couldn't do anything about the biggest point of my dysphoria, which was my chest. Being able to have top surgery was very important to me and helped massively with my dysphoria, but until surgery, binding my chest and wearing certain clothes helped me feel better.

After I'd been on testosterone and had top surgery, I'd say my dysphoria reduced by a good 80 per cent, and it continued to be helped by the further changes caused by testosterone. Bottom/lower (genital) dysphoria was always a background thing for me personally, but I know it's wildly different for others. I initially wasn't sure about bottom surgery, so I took my time enjoying the new freedom and relief I felt in my body from hormones and top surgery, and waited several years before pursuing bottom surgery.

My lower dysphoria crept in over time, but despite this, the boost in confidence, self-esteem and comfort I felt in my body after I'd had bottom surgery took me completely by surprise. I felt complete, and like the weight of pushing through my transition, through the waiting lists and the roadblocks and the transphobia, had all been worth it. I finally felt fully at peace with who I was, both internally and socially.

My dysphoria now is a once-in-a-blue-moon occurrence, rather than a constant daily barrage of extreme discomfort. It's like a little whack-a-mole popping up every now and again, and I just quickly bop it back down.

DID ANY STEPS OF SOCIALLY OR MEDICALLY TRANSITIONING IMPACT YOUR DYSPHORIA?

'Having my name and pronouns used always feels amazing. Not getting misgendered is huge.'

R, 30, trans man/non-binary

'Laser hair removal produced visible results that helped my dysphoria, and the physical effects of HRT have helped significantly. Also friends and colleagues respecting my new name and pronouns have been a huge confidence boost and give me strong feelings of euphoria.'

Eve, 26, trans woman

'Actively trying to be read as a man made me a bit more aware of my physical dysphoria, but my voice dropping definitely helped.'

Ian, 21, transgender man

'Oh, for sure, testosterone and my top surgery had the biggest impact. Testosterone made my feelings and reactions make sense, and my top surgery literally and metaphorically lifted a weight off my chest.'

Lesley, 30, genderqueer/non-binary

'Being able to have gender-affirming surgeries, and legally changing my name and gender marker, reduced my dysphoria significantly.'

Sanjay, 30, transgender man

'Socially and medically transitioning impacted a lot! I feel so much better, and I haven't been suicidal since.'

Milo, 24, trans man

The Funny(?) Bits

I think it's fair to say this has been a pretty heavy chapter! Dysphoria is definitely one of the heaviest and darkest things to deal with when transitioning, so I want to round off this part with some of the funnier aspects and silver linings to an otherwise stormy cloud! It's important to be able to laugh things off, and it helps to reclaim some power over the nasty dysphoria beast.

I'll kick us off:

- One time I found myself getting triggered by my fingernails. Literally the shape and appearance of my fingernails. HOW STUPID IS THAT. Nobody else cares what my fingernails looks like - big oof. Fingernail dysphoria (omg) gradually faded away throughout my transition. But yeah, there you go: fingernails!

- Understanding dysphoria definitely helped me communicate my feelings to my friends and family a lot better. Yay for unexpected self-growth and developed socialising skills!

- Sometimes I'd be super up for getting *down*, if you know what I mean, and dysphoria would rear its ugly little head at the worst time. After saying my random codeword, we'd pop a movie on and just not talk for a bit. Imagine what that must have looked like! I can just envisage my younger self sitting there, watching some Disney film with Shaaba thinking, *Damn you, Nemo, you stupid little cock-blocking fish …*

- When I look back at the arguments I started or moods I found myself in when triggered with dysphoria, it almost felt like those Snickers adverts – the ones that say: 'You're not you when you're hungry – get some nuts.' Imagine if it was: 'You're not you when you're dysphoric – get some nuts.' If only it were that easy, Snickers. IF ONLY.

WHAT WERE SOME OF YOUR 'FUNNY' OR 'WEIRD' DYSPHORIA TRIGGERS THAT YOU CAN NOW LAUGH ABOUT?

'My toes make me dysphoric sometimes. I look at them and think, *Those are girly toes*, and then I slap myself in the face and ask how a bloody toe can be girly. Toes are just an example, but sometimes the silliest, minutest things make me dysphoric, ha-ha.'

George, 18, trans man

'I was once dysphoric about my trouser buttons … somehow my mind convinced me that they were too shiny-gold. I thought bronze or silver buttons would look more masculine?!'

Leander, 18, trans man

'I never pack in public, despite having bulge-related dysphoria, because I knew someone whose packer flopped out of the stall in a men's room!'

Melvin, 27, trans man

'I used to have a very hard time taking baths. I used colourful bath bombs so I couldn't see my body under the water that well. It really helped – until I started having intrusive thoughts about sea monsters in my bathtub!!!'

Alice, 21, trans man

Gender dysphoria is tough, but it does get easier. While it might feel totally hopeless in the moment, know that the waves will pass, and they'll also get smaller and less frequent. There are many more amazing moments you'll experience as you go through your transition and live as who you know you are. Pretty soon, you'll be able to stare your dysphoria in the face and give it the middle finger.

6

WHAT IS SOCIALLY TRANSITIONING?

'Incredible. It felt like I was finally being
seen for the first time.'

Asher, 23, AFAB non-binary

So you've discovered the word 'transgender', realised
that's who you are, told everyone and been intro-
duced to the troll that is dysphoria. I'm happy to tell you
that this next step is the first step of the rest of your life.
Look at me being a fortune cookie.

First things first: what do I even mean by 'socially
transitioning'? Simply put, this is the process whereby a
trans person begins living and presenting socially (and
privately) as their true gender. It can be done fully, as in
full-time all the time, or in certain contexts (for example
some trans people might be out to their friends and
certain family members, but not at work).

In this chapter we're going to go through all the steps
of socially transitioning, from what you wear to legally
changing your name.

The essence of socially transitioning is changing your
name and pronouns more widely. For me, this meant

living and presenting as a man, using he/him pronouns, and introducing myself as Jamie. Good times. Very good times actually! Each time I heard 'Jamie', or was referred to using he/him pronouns, gave me a sparkly little moment of trans joy. Whether it was a cashier saying, 'Would you like a bag, sir?' or my mum talking to someone and saying 'my son'. He-he. It was a stark contrast to the discomfort of being referred to incorrectly (deadname and she/her pronouns), and it was GREAT.

HOW DID IT FEEL TO BE CORRECTLY GENDERED WHEN SOCIALLY TRANSITIONING?

'*Amazing*. It validated my presence and where I was, and showed me that some people cared to listen to my needs as a person.'

Rowen, 18, trans man/masc

'Honestly, it felt like comfort. It was the absence of pain. At first, I was thrilled each time. Now I'm just comfortable.'

Charlie, 28, woman (trans woman/intersex)

'I feel so happy, but sometimes I worry that people still see me as a woman even when using the right pronouns.'

Jess, 25, non-binary

'It felt like the sound a Mario Kart character makes when they get a prize: WAHOO! Even now, when it's someone new, it's so nice!'

Jamie, 20, trans man

'Pure euphoria. The first time it happened, I burst into a fit of giggles. It was even funnier when I saw the confused face of the old woman who had just called me a young girl!'

Amity, 18, trans woman

Socially transitioning can also involve taking active steps in changing your appearance, changing your legal identity, and simply coming out more widely and introducing yourself as the real you. There's a whole bunch of things that trans people can do at this stage, which can be done in any combination that feels right for them.

Why Is Socially Transitioning Important?

These are the first major affirming steps you take that are not just private and for yourself. This is where you get to publicly reflect who you are inside. Despite this being described as a public display of who you are, it's not something that trans people do for others, it's something they do for themselves.

You might have heard the term 'passing'. It's a phrase that has a rocky history among the trans community and is used less as times goes on. Passing is the act of being read as your true gender by society. When you're catching the bus and the driver says 'Thanks, man,' you'd be passing as a man on that occasion.

The term can put a lot of pressure on trans people to feel a need to always 'pass', or to satisfy particular stereotypes that might not authentically fit them. It also implies that trans people are passing themselves off as something, rather than *being* that something.

Passing is never a primary reason for somebody to socially transition. The important reasons are reducing dysphoria and prioritising safety, particularly when accessing gendered spaces. But passing can often be something that in and of itself reduces dysphoria. It's affirming to hear people around you respond to a true reflection of yourself, and it's okay to acknowledge and embrace this, as long as you're doing it for you, not for society.

What About Gendered Spaces?

One context that 'passing' feels most important for is gendered spaces. Public toilets and changing rooms are another couple of trolls that you'll encounter. They can be intimidating spaces to access, and it's not always easy to know which gendered space you should use during the early stages of your transition. At the end of the day, I know that all I wanted to do was pee, or try on some clothes, but unfortunately wider discussions about trans people have turned peeing into a rather political issue (#FreeThePee).

The number one thing to keep in mind as a trans person is your safety when accessing public gendered spaces. In an ideal world, trans people should use the correct gendered spaces as soon as they come out, but it's not always that easy if not being read as your correct gender could make you unsafe.

I was frequently receiving odd looks and occasional comments when using the women's public toilets, even before I realised I was trans. This meant it was an obvious decision for me to immediately start using men's public spaces as soon as I came out, as I felt safe to do so. But everyone's journey will be different. For some trans people, there may also be an awkward limbo phase in being gendered correctly, with odd looks regardless of which gendered space you use.

At the end of the day, the decision is yours to make for when you feel is most appropriate for you to access the correctly gendered spaces for you. It might even be that gendered spaces are never a place that you feel safe in. In these scenarios, gender-neutral spaces can be true heroes. (There are great apps out there to help you locate these spaces in your local area – more info in the Resources section!)

So What Steps Fall Under Socially Transitioning?

Think about anything and everything that could change in your life that doesn't require hormones and surgery but would be gender-affirming to you, and that's basically what you can do to socially transition.

The more definitive steps for socially transitioning include: using a new name and different pronouns, public profiles and legalities, hair, clothing, binding and packing (for the trans mascs) and padding and tucking (for the trans femmes). Let's go through these in turn.

Name and Pronouns

The most obvious thing to mention is your new name and pronouns. We had a chat about choosing these back in Chapter 2, but at this stage it's also about *sharing* your name and pronouns with everyone (or as many people as you want/need to).

When asking people to switch the name and pronouns they use for you, it's important to accept that there will almost always be slip-ups at the beginning. Think about how long you've been using your birthname and old pronouns. It'll take time for people to learn, even if they're trying their best. My parents took a good year to stop making mistakes. I found that framing it in my mind as a habit that people needed to change helped me to not get so frustrated.

☆ **Top Tip:** *Some trans people like to wear pronoun accessories to help remind those around them what pronouns to use. These could be badges, wristbands, lanyards or pendants that clearly state 'she/her', 'he/him', 'they/them', etc. Cute and functional.*

♥ **For the Allies:** *It's okay if you slip up with someone's new name and pronouns while you're getting used to them. It can feel frustrating for you to make these mistakes, especially if you can immediately see your trans loved one feeling hurt or uncomfortable because of your mistake. You might think that apologising multiple times can help a trans person understand it was an honest mistake, but this often leads to more* *discomfort, especially in public. The best thing to do if you accidentally misgender somebody is to quickly correct yourself and move on. – Shaaba*

Public Profiles and Legalities

Once you have your new name and pronouns, it's natural to want to share them. There are channels where you can *choose* to share, like social media profiles or on your library card (do people still use library cards?!). There might also be channels where you *need* to share, like at school or in your workplace, with your bank and on legal documents.

It can seem overwhelming, especially when there are often specific processes for changing your name and pronouns that vary depending on the institution or where you live. Nobody likes dealing with a lot of paperwork and it can often be boring – but silver lining, you'll get your new signature down!

To help make it less overwhelming for you, here's a list of a lot of the main things you'll want to update after changing your name. If you're the kind of person who likes to write in books, there are even cute little boxes you can tick once you've done all the ones relevant to you!

☐ Driving licence
☐ Passport
☐ Bank accounts
☐ Credit cards
☐ Finance/loan companies
☐ Pension

☐ Utility bills (water, electricity, gas, internet)
☐ Local authority (council tax and electoral register)

- [ ] Insurance providers (e.g. car insurance)
- [ ] Student ID cards (and your place of education too, obviously)
- [ ] Travel cards, such as railcards
- [ ] PayPal (sounds silly, but it's one I forgot about and it was an awkward moment the next time I sent money)
- [ ] Social media
- [ ] Email accounts
- [ ] Your employer
- [ ] Doctor
- [ ] Dentist
- [ ] Mortgage provider
- [ ] House deeds/landlord and tenancy agreements
- [ ] Mobile phone provider
- [ ] Streaming services
- [ ] Subscriptions and newsletters
- [ ] Tax office

☆ **Top Tip:** *Try to be as comprehensive as possible when changing your name and gender marker. This isn't just for your comfort, but because it logistically helps to avoid issues that might occur if you have different names on different documents.*

Some of the above can be changed before you legally change your name, like your social media accounts, but most will require proof of a legal name change before updating. In the UK to change things like your passport requires not just evidence of legally changing your name, but also a letter from your doctor or a medical professional confirming that your 'change' of gender is permanent – their phrasing, not mine. The most common place to request these is from a doctor you see at a gender clinic. This letter is required because you're also able to update your gender marker on these documents.

You might notice that birth certificate is missing from the above list, and that's because, in the UK at least, to change your birth certificate you need a Gender Recognition Certificate (GRC) which requires more than a deed poll to obtain. If you're outside of the UK, however, please do check the rules for where you live, as you may be able to change your birth certificate more simply.

A Gender Recognition Certificate is also a legal document, but typically not one that you'd look to get at the stage of social transitioning. It was actually the last thing I did as part of my transition, and I'll go through it more in Chapter 12 (but again, do check for differences if you're not in the UK).

Let's Get Hairy

Getting a haircut or a wig is often such a MOMENT for trans people that it's become a whole thing. You might have seen videos of other trans people, typically trans masculine people, getting their hair cut from long to short all in one go. If you haven't, I'd recommend checking them out, they're pretty sweet. But why is a haircut such a big deal? And why is it connected to socially transitioning?

Well, in part, it's because hair is still seen as a very gendered thing. We're all aware that anyone of any gender can have any length or style of hair, but for a trans person in the early stages of transition, having a haircut more typical for their gender (or in line with their gender expression) can make a huge difference in reducing dysphoria and increasing confidence.

With my hair I never went for *the chop*; I was always too nervous to cut it all off in one go. Instead, I went from shoulder-length to this odd chin-length bob (no, I didn't want to speak to the manager). Then came the Bieber sweep, and eventually I got the back and sides shaved very short and actively asked for a 'masculine' haircut. Although I didn't go for getting rid of it all in one go, which a lot of people do, I still felt a growing confidence with each step – or rather, each cut.

For trans women or trans feminine people, growing your hair out, switching up a hairstyle, or using wigs or hair extensions can be an incredibly affirming change.

DID YOU CHANGE YOUR HAIRSTYLE AS PART OF YOUR TRANSITION?

'I've grown my hair out a lot and dyed it many different colours to experiment with it. I've also bought a bunch of cool wigs, which I love.'

Gwyndolin, 21, trans woman

'I let my hair grow out. It took a while to get to a place where I like it, but now it feels amazing.'

Eve, 26, trans woman

As hairstyles are seen as very gendered, changing your hair can make a big difference to your appearance, thus can potentially help a lot with other people gendering you correctly and using your correct pronouns, as well as the small deal of how you feel about yourself – you know, that tiny matter of self-esteem and feeling more confident. Pffft.

What to Wear

Clothes. Another thing that's still heavily gendered by society. Which is silly, really, considering pink clothing and make-up were encouraged for men in the past. And have you *seen* Mel Gibson in *Braveheart*?! People can look great in any clothes, and it's a heavily Western stereotype that men wear trousers and women wear dresses. You can wear whatever you want, and your clothes can be typical for your gender, or not. You're a trans guy who wants to wear dresses? Go for it! You're a trans woman who doesn't want to wear dresses? Awesome! And if you're non-binary, you don't need to present androgynously!

Equally, there's nothing wrong with wearing clothing that's typical for your gender identity. A majority of trans men will wear more stereotypically masculine clothing, and a majority of trans women will wear more stereotypically feminine clothing. Wear whatever you want to wear, basically. Completely change up your wardrobe after coming out, or keep it exactly the same as before. You do you.

I personally changed over my wardrobe quite gradually before I even knew I was trans, from 'girl' clothes to 'boy' clothes, as I realised that's what I was more comfortable with. When I first came out and started living as Jamie, I got rid of the last of my 'girl' clothes because that's what I wanted to do at the time. Now, though, a good chunk of my wardrobe is from the women's section in clothing stores. I personally don't wear skirts or dresses, but I love the way certain sweatshirts and blouses from women's sections look on me. I definitely buy what I like and don't pay attention to where it's from, but in the early days, I strongly rejected anything that might mean people would misgender me, which meant shunning anything remotely 'feminine'. I think a lot of people re-explore their style throughout their transition, and it can happen multiple times!

ARE THERE ANY CLOTHING HACKS THAT HELPED YOU DURING YOUR TRANSITION?

'As a trans guy, I like going for a simple but fashionable boxy style, with oversized T-shirts, hoodies, jackets layered on top of each other, and tighter bottoms, and big chunky shoes.'

R, 30, trans man/non-binary

'As a trans woman, wearing two pairs of pants helps with tucking, or reducing visibility when I wear tighter trousers or shorts.'

Eve, 26, trans woman

'Get pyjamas that feel good! I often feel dysphoric in the evening when not binding, so I like to wear PJs that make me feel good and a thick fluffy dressing gown !

Jamie, 20, trans man

'As someone who is trans femme, I found pairing a corset belt with a nice dress is a great way of adding more curvature to my body. It feels so good!'

Matt, 26, trans femme enby

'As a trans man, I find that wearing simple band rings help reduce hand dysphoria, and thick-sole shoes help to increase my height.'

Luan, 20, trans man

Binding

Trans masc people will often bind to further masculin-ise their appearance in clothes. It's the process of using material to create the appearance of a flatter chest – I say flatter, because everybody's shape is different and even cis guys don't have a totally flat chest, so keep this in mind when binding! There's so much information about binding and it's important that you do your own research thoroughly before giving it a go.

Safety always comes first.

A binder is essentially a tight-fitting vest that's thicker at the front to compress the chest. I won't lie: binding sucks. It's uncomfortable, tight and restrictive. It's also freeing. I remember the first time I used a binder and saw a flat chest under my T-shirt in the mirror. It just felt ... right. I felt relief and euphoria, which didn't just help my internal dysphoria, but also helped me feel more comfortable in public.

HOW DID IT FEEL TO BIND FOR THE FIRST TIME?

'Amazing! I felt so happy to finally see myself how I should be, and to wear clothes more comfortably. It felt really freeing.'

Taryn, 18, trans man

'Amazing, I almost cried looking at myself in the mirror, as I looked how I felt I should.'

Asher, 23, AFAB non-binary

'Physically uncomfortable. It took days for my body to adjust. But after that it felt nice to see how flat my chest was. The compression of the vest never felt great though, so after a year I switched to a non-padded sports bra. That really helped me get through high school.'

Rowen, 18, trans man/masc

A lot of people call me a 'trans-dad' online, and when it comes to safety I'll happily step into that role! So if you're considering binding, please make sure you read this advice **very carefully** before you embark on any binding journey. I know how important it is to feel flatter chested, but it's not worth damaging your health.

- There are different types of binders, but you should **never use more than one**, or buy them in smaller sizes – this won't make them work better.

- For people who can't access binders (due to affordability or being closeted) there are DIY ways to bind safely, including layering clothes, and wearing sports bras or sports compression shirts. **Never use duct tape or compression bandages.** They restrict your breathing rather than moving with your body, and could cause serious (and sometimes permanent) harm.

- **The maximum time for binding is 8–10 hours**, preferably with small breaks in between. You also shouldn't bind for this long every single day. Listen to your body: if your maximum is 6 hours, respect that.

- Only wear your binder while you're awake, **never sleep in a binder**. Not even for a little nap, and not even if you've not worn one during the day.

- Try not to bind when exercising, or if the weather is really hot. If you have to, be careful, keep hydrated and don't push yourself.

- If you have respiratory issues, like asthma, it's crucial that you seek medical advice before binding.

- Binding isn't comfortable, but **it shouldn't cause you pain**. If it does, stop immediately. You may need a larger binder, or to seek medical advice if pain persists.

Binding incorrectly can lead to broken ribs and permanent damage, so it's super important that you're safe.

Now, please stick out your little finger and pinky-promise me that you'll bind safely.

☆ **Top Tip:** *I would highly recommend watching video tutorials on how to put on a binder before giving it a go. They're not like regular tops. Yes, I've put my arm through the head hole and gotten stuck before, and you probably will too!*

💜 **For the Allies:** *I struggled to see Jamie voluntarily endure the pain and discomfort of binding. It took me a while to realise that without binding, his internal pain and discomfort was far greater. There is a balance to be struck of supporting binding, and kindly pointing out if your trans loved one is physically struggling to breathe, or if they've been binding for too long. If they don't respond well, remind them that you're only putting their safety first. Sometimes I offered to leave Jamie alone, as he felt more comfortable removing his binder when he was by himself. Perhaps a similar suggestion might help your trans loved one too. – Shaaba*

Packing  trans masc

No, we're not talking about suitcases here, we're talking *penises*. Packing, put simply, is creating a bulge in your pants. Just like binding, this can be done using something official, called a packer, or DIY (think a rolled-up sock – I heard of someone using a condom full of lube once but that got very messy!). Some people crochet their own penis, which looks as adorable as it sounds, to be honest.

Packers come in all shapes and sizes, even skin tones and functions. There's really a lot of choice when it comes to picking a penis – and you can have multiple! The most common packer is a squishy silicone penis that looks semi-realistic.

☆ **Top Tip:** *It can be very tempting to go large when choosing the size of your penis, but trust me that something around 3–4 inches will work much better for packing. Larger packers run the risk of making it look like you have a permanent boner. You have been warned.*

The other functions of packers almost act as upgrades beyond just looking like a dick. There are stand-to-pee (STP) packers, which do what they say on the tin. They allow users to pee standing up through a hole at the base that you position against yourself, so the pee travels through the packer. Cis women use basic STPs, the biggest known brand being 'She-Wee' (terrible name, I know). For trans masc people, STPs can allow you to pee at public urinals, as there aren't many toilet stalls in men's public restrooms. The ability to stand up while peeing can be incredibly affirming and dysphoria-reducing for many people, but it does take practice to make sure you're not left with pee-covered trousers.

Another type of functional packers are pack-and-play devices. These tend to be more realistic, but can also get very pricey. These allow users to have penetrative sex with a packer (remember that fully informed consent is both sexy and important!).

Packing doesn't come with the same safety tips as binding as it's not as dangerous if you don't do it prop- erly – though it can lead to some awkward situations. Penis falling down your trouser leg, anyone? How about jumping into a swimming pool, and suddenly ... *no penis*.

There are a few things you can do to secure a packer in place: harnesses; underwear with specific packing pouches; safely pinning DIY penis pouches to underwear (very safely ...); wearing a second pair of pants; a good old shave-and-glue (the shaving helps to avoid any unsched- uled waxing). There are a lot of options to explore in the world of packing – go nuts! He-he.

Padding

It's normal (and healthy) for us all to have different body shapes and proportions, but there are body shapes that are seen as being more typically masculine or feminine. Padding can help AMAB trans people achieve a more stereotypically feminine body shape, mostly through accentuating the hips and breasts. Most people have heard of padding because of drag queens who use padding on their hips and bums to change their shoul- der-to-hip ratio in often greatly exaggerated ways, but padding can also be done more subtly. You can also pad bras, and can even get bras with little pockets in them for prosthetic breasts.

HOW DOES PADDING MAKE YOU FEEL?

'I have a sports bra that I put socks down. It feels natural and right. I get euphoric when I notice, but a lot of the time, it just feels comfy and correct.'

Matt, 26, trans femme enby

Tucking

Tucking is the opposite of packing, where instead of *creating* a bulge, it's making a bulge visually disappear. AMAB trans people often do this to flatten their genital region for a more feminine-typical look.

HOW DOES TUCKING MAKE YOU FEEL?

'I love it. I hate the look of a bulge, and I hate the feeling of it moving. It's gone when it is stowed!'

Charlie, 28, woman (trans woman/intersex)

'I don't often tuck, as most of my clothes are flowy or over-sized. With some tighter dresses, I'll tuck to get a more feminine figure. It just feels correct, if a little uncomfortable.'

Matt, 26, trans femme enby

'I tucked once for a photoshoot and never again, because it felt like it wasn't really me. I was very body-conscious, especially down there, but it was very uncomfortable and in some ways, I didn't feel that I needed to hide that part of me. It was part of my journey, and the fact I was pre-op was just a step in my process.'

Veronica, 37, trans woman

Generally speaking, tucking involves pushing the penis back between the legs and securing it in place. Like binding, this process can be a little uncomfortable at first, but shouldn't be painful, and should always be done safely.

There are a few different ways of tucking, including tight underwear. This is often seen as the easiest and most comfortable option, and can include athletic underwear or trans-specific underwear. Underwear is also the least secure way of tucking and increases the potential of things slipping out of place.

Similar to underwear, but designed specifically for tucking, are gaffs. These are a type of sturdy underwear that typically have a bit of padding in the front to give a flattened presence. Gaffs are more secure than standard underwear due to the padding but can also feel or look a little bulky.

Finally, tape is seen as the most secure way to tuck, but is also considered the most uncomfortable and has the potential to leave tape-glue residue. If you're considering tape to tuck, make sure that you use medical tape, as other types may cause pain or injury. It's important to also consider bathroom breaks during the time you'd be tucking with tape, and to plan ahead – it's not as simple to take on and off as underwear is!

Phew.

That was a lot to run through! That's it for the major bits and pieces that are considered part of socially transitioning. Remember, you don't have to do anything on this list, or you might want to do everything on this list.

The essence of socially transitioning is living as your true self, your true gender. There's no requirement to change the way you dress or have your hair. You don't have to bind, pack, tuck or pad anything. I personally used to bind before I had top surgery, but I only dabbled once or twice with packing – it just wasn't for me. You do what affirms your gender to you, and what makes you happy and comfortable (or as happy and comfortable as possible).

The only requirement you might experience is if you want to change your name, as you'll have to do this legally for it to be on certain documents.

7

HORMONES – THE GOOD, THE BAD AND THE SURPRISING

'Hello, my name is Jamie and this is my
voice three months on T!'

It's hormone time (sounds like the worst superhero catchphrase ever). Hormones are often the first medical step trans people will take in their transition. For trans youth the first step may be puberty blockers (also known as hormone blockers, or gonadotropin-releasing hormone agonists if you want to get fancy about it). We'll have a quick chat about these, and then dive into the more traditional hormones that make up HRT (hormone replacement therapy).

💜 **For the Allies:** *HRT sounds like a big and scary thing. While it is a huge step, it's also safe, and it's some-thing that thousands of people have gone through, including cis people. HRT is commonly prescribed to cis women who have hormone imbalances for other reasons, like polycystic ovary syndrome (which affects about 1 in 10 cis women in the UK), or as a way to* *manage menopause. It's also prescribed to cis men who need testicles removed (following certain cancers, for example), or those who have naturally low testosterone levels. It can sometimes help with any overwhelming feelings you have around your trans loved one taking hormones, to know how commonly HRT is taken in a range of contexts. – Shaaba*

Puberty Blockers

Like HRT, puberty blockers have been used for quite a while in different contexts, including in precocious puberty (when puberty begins too early) in cisgender kids, and for trans kids to avoid irreversible puberty that increases dysphoria. Puberty blockers are hormone agonists that essentially block testicles from making testosterone and ovaries from making oestrogen and progesterone.

When taken pre-adolescence, they essentially put a pause on puberty from happening, which for trans kids means they don't need to go through the wrong puberty for their true gender. This can drastically decrease feelings of gender dysphoria, and reduce the number of procedures and surgeries needed later on (for example, a trans man wouldn't need top surgery if puberty blockers had stopped his chest from growing, and a trans woman wouldn't need vocal-changing procedures or training if her voice had never broken).

As with accessing hormones, there will be a lot of waiting and talking to specialists before trans youth may be offered puberty blockers - they're not handed out quickly or easily. When trans youth are able to access blockers, they really do lead to improved wellbeing,[1] and importantly: their effects are **reversible**.[2]

Unfortunately, puberty blockers have become a contentious news topic due to transphobic people and press, who simply don't like the fact that trans kids exist. As with any medication, puberty blockers can have side-effects, including hot flushes and fatigue, but usage is monitored carefully and frequently, medication is altered or stopped if issues occur, and they are physically reversible with positive psychological effects found consistently.

HRT

Regardless of puberty blockers, trans people use HRT to correct their hormone balance in a way that reflects their true gender. For trans masc people, that involves taking testosterone, also known as 'T'. For trans femme people, that involves taking oestrogen, also known as 'E' (it's sometimes spelled 'estrogen' without the silent 'o' – just go with it).

Now when I say 'the good, the bad and the surprising' of hormones, these will differ depending on who you ask. Some trans masc people really look forward to getting

---

1 'Mental Health Outcomes in Transgender and Nonbinary Youths Receiving Gender-Affirming Care' (2022), Tordoff, Wanta, Collin et al., *JAMA* Network Open; 'Pubertal Suppression for Transgender Youth and Risk of Suicidal Ideation' (2022), Turban, King, Carswell and Keuroghlian, *Pediatrics*
2 Gender Identity Development Service: Puberty and physical intervention (https://gids.nhs.uk/young-people/puberty-and-physical-intervention/)

hairier, while others consider it more of a nuisance! As with many things, there's a lot more depth to the world of hormones than we can cover in this chapter, but I've linked to some great resources at the end of this book if you're interested in exploring further.

💜 **For the Allies:** *Jamie was super excited to take hormones, and while I was happy for him, a part of me was also nervous. I didn't want certain aspects of Jamie to change, and having little understanding of HRT, I worried that making him more 'manly' would also mean changing his gender expression. As silly as it sounds, I thought taking T would make Jamie angry, less considerate, maybe tougher. Looking back, it almost sounds like I was worried he'd turn into a football-and-beer-obsessed lads' lad overnight! None of these things happened, as the traits people have in that sense are more to do with nurture than nature. HRT didn't change who Jamie was, but it gave him the comfort and confidence to be a greater version of himself. Jamie was still Jamie: taking T just made him Jamie x 100. – Shaaba*

Regardless of whether you're taking T or E, it's important to remember that hormones can change a lot, and there are some things they can never change. They can also change different things in different ways, at different times, for different people. You can't pick and choose the changes caused by hormones. Typically, HRT takes at least three months to start creating noticeable changes. They'll work according to your genetics and dose, and you can't be in control of what changes happen, when they happen and to what extent they happen.

While this might be disappointing to hear for some, it reflects what would happen if you were cis. No cis man chooses how full his beard grows in, and no cis woman chooses her voice. You shouldn't look to HRT as something that will bring about very specific changes; it's about replicating the puberty you should have had the first time around (and no one can control what the outcome will be!).

People often talk about the physical changes caused by hormones, but there are emotional ones as well. You won't turn into a different person, but remember how it was going through puberty for the first time? (Or maybe the only time, if you're a cis person reading this!) You're basically going through being that person again, but with different hormones this time, so you'll also experience mood swings and changes in your emotions, just as you probably did the first time around.

If you want to continue experiencing the effects of HRT and maintaining changes, you'll have to keep taking it forever. Similarly, anyone (cis or trans) who has had reproductive organs removed will need to stay on HRT for the rest of their lives. Some people may choose to come off HRT for a variety of reasons, and this can be temporary (to have fertility treatment, for example). Many of the changes caused by hormones are permanent, but there are many that aren't, and these will reverse, at least to some extent, if you stop taking them. Trans masc people who stop taking testosterone will likely experience periods again. Similarly, trans femme people who stop taking oestrogen will likely notice an increase in body and facial hair.

☆ **Top Tip:** *Some people think that taking extra hormones can encourage changes to happen faster, or make more change happen. This isn't true. You shouldn't be taking a higher dose of hormones than you've been medically advised too, as having high levels of a hormone can cause certain side-effects, including excess testosterone converting to oestrogen!*

☆ **Top Tip:** *You should never take black-market hormones, ever. I understand waiting times can suck. You know what would suck more? Getting seriously ill from unregulated medication, and then getting in trouble on top of that. It'll be so worth the wait to do this right. Safety always comes first.*

When Does This Happen?

As a trans man, I knew I needed testosterone, but the process for starting HRT is similar regardless of whether you're a trans man, a trans woman or non-binary. I started my journey to hormones in mid-2011, when I was 17.

I had no idea where to start. Literally none. I watched YouTube videos of all the trans guys I could find, but they were all based in the USA. I searched online endlessly, and still didn't understand what I could do. The process is a lot clearer now, thankfully, and a quick Google search can point you in the right direction! I eventually found out I had to speak to my GP (that's General Practitioner, a local doctor for those of you who might be unfamiliar with British lingo).

'Hello GP, please help me understand what to do.' That was the gist of my conversation. My GP knew how the referral process to gender identity clinics (GICs) worked. At the time, you needed a referral to have an appointment with a local mental health service first, who would then do the actual referral to a GIC, if they decided that was appropriate. Nowadays, GPs can refer straight to GICs.

This is one way that the process has got easier in recent years, but there's still a 'luck of the draw' when it comes to doctors. A long-straw doctor is accepting, knowledge-able, and has had trans-specific training and experience with previous trans patients. While this should be the standard, it's still quite uncommon. Some doctors might be willing to help you, but have no idea how. My current doctor is like this. In these cases, be confident and honest about how you feel, and come prepared with credible information that can help your doctor know what to do next. It might be that you need to walk them through the referral process (which isn't ideal, but at least it gets you where you need to go). Drawing the short straw may match you with a doctor who isn't trans-friendly, and who may even refuse to refer you to a GIC in the first place. If you're worried this is the case, try to bring someone sup-portive with you to your appointment, and remember that there should be appeal processes and alternative doctors that you can speak with.

I was *so* lucky to have drawn a long straw with my doctor. But then came the waiting list information: uh-oh. It would be at least six months to see the mental health service, and then at least 18 months from that appointment to have an initial appointment with the GIC, and then there would be at least six months between each appointment (with an undisclosed number of appointments being needed) before I would get approved for hormones. This meant I was looking at a minimum of two and a half years.

My heart sank. It felt like I was being told that my life would be paused for all that time until I could finally get the medical support I needed. Remember that lovely beast dysphoria? In that moment of hearing how long it would take, I thought of all of the things I was dysphoric about. Having to wait so long to have any relief from that felt impossible. Writing this book, I questioned whether to explain how I felt in that moment. It wasn't a great feeling, and waiting lists are the same now, sometimes even longer, than the two and a half years I was told. Some people have to wait five years until they can have their very first appointment. Not hormones, but the first step towards them. It's important to share just how abysmal trans healthcare waiting lists are, at least in the UK. It absolutely needs to change.

I went home and instantly searched online for alternatives. Now that I knew they were called GICs, I could search for different options, and that's when I found out there were private clinics. I realise how incredibly privileged I am that my family supported me in paying for private treatment. It made the process significantly quicker, and I understand not everybody is able to do this.

In August 2011, I made an appointment with a private clinic. The waiting list was only a couple of weeks, and I was offered an appointment in September. After my first appointment with a specialist doctor, I was asked to live full-time as my gender for three months. That was the clinic's minimum time period to make sure I was consistent with being Jamie, and was sure that this was what I had to do. I'd been Jamie for several months already, but the doctor took my official date from when I legally changed my name. My second GIC appointment was in January 2012, and as a private patient I could book the required counselling session for the same day. My approval for hormones was given that same day as well, and I started HRT three weeks later on 25 January 2012. Less than four months. Private clinics today have longer waiting lists, and typically longer requirements for living as your gender. All this to say: the public system *really* needs to change.

Testosterone

Testosterone comes as a gel, as injections or as patches, with injections being the most common. I started on a gel form and stayed on this for the first year, before switching to a slow-release injection that I got every 12 weeks for a few years, and then went back to gel. The method of application is all down to individual preference. Gel seems more inconvenient because it needs to be applied every day, and you need to avoid skin-to-skin contact for a while, but it keeps your hormone levels the most consistent. You only need to think about slow-release injections every 12 weeks, but they're a pain in the butt (literally), and can lead to low levels just before and just after administration. Swings and roundabouts.

Changes from testosterone can take a while to start appearing, and then BAM! you have the world's hairiest butt crack. Or at least that's what it can feel like. You think I'm kidding, but I was desperate for a beard and all I got for the first three years was a progressively hairier butt (among other things). Testosterone tends to have less subtle changes than oestrogen has. There's a lot more irreversible/very-difficult-to-reverse changes (e.g. when your voice breaks, it can't unbreak) and it can change *a lot*.

The most common changes include a deeper voice, increased facial and body hair growth, fat redistribution to a more typically 'masculine' shape, genital growth, the stopping of periods, an increase in muscle mass and strength, oilier skin, acne, the thinning of head hair, vein prominence, increased perspiration, a stronger body and urine odour, and increased sex drive. And ... breathe. There are things that T won't change, like the bone structure of your hips, your height, and the level of breast tissue you have.

The change I was most excited about was my voice dropping, which happened noticeably at about three months on testosterone – this was the point I got called 'the squeaky chicken'. Voice breaks can be very embarrassing, especially when you're at an age when no other guy is experiencing them anymore. I'd shout a friend's name to get their attention, and my voice would do that funny *uhUHuhUHHuhh* thing. Awkward.

My body hair started coming in properly from about six months; yes, starting with the butt hair. Then some stomach and leg hair. My chest and facial hair took YEARS to come in, even a little bit. I had to muster all my patience to wait for this!

Fat redistribution was a slow burner and happened gradually for the first several years, but overall T has changed how I look drastically. My face, body, hair (gain and loss), voice, muscle mass and tone, smell (which is so much worse now, ha-ha) and weight. Even my fingers are thicker than they used to be.

But despite all these physical changes, the biggest change *by far* has been psychological.

I'm a happier, more confident version of myself. I felt more at home in my skin within a few months, and never looked back. This was absolutely the right thing for me to do, and I am so grateful I was able to do it.

Oestrogen

Oestrogen comes in the form of pills, a gel, patches or injections, but pills and injections are typically the more popular methods. Anti-androgens can also be taken to hold back the effects of testosterone, allowing oestrogen to work to its maximum effect.

Generally, the effects of oestrogen are more subtle than testosterone. One of the reasons for this is because testosterone causes a lot of irreversible physical changes. Someone's voice can't unbreak, but it can be trained to sound higher. Facial hair might thin, but it won't completely go away without laser treatment. Bone structural changes from testosterone can't be reversed, but body fat redistribution can alter body shape quite a lot.

Oestrogen can cause some pretty great, dysphoria-butt-kicking changes, including: body fat redistribution, decreased muscle mass and strength, body and facial hair thinning (and slower growth), breast growth, head-hair-loss reduction, skin softening, oil reduction, and decreased sperm, libido and erections.

Luxeria is a 33-year-old trans woman from the UK with a degree in biochemistry, and a brilliant YouTube channel where she talks about plastic surgery, beauty and more. Luxeria has kindly shared her experience with taking oestrogen (and also of breast augmentation, which you can find in the next chapter).

LUXERIA

There are several pathways for male-to-female HRT. Anti-androgen injections (to suppress testosterone) can be taken alongside oestrogen, which will be administered orally or sublingually (both in the form of pills), or as a transdermal gel, or as injections or patches. Some people experience much faster or more stable results from sublingual pills, injections or patches, but typically pills taken orally or transdermal gels are what are prescribed on UK public healthcare.

There are also other methods of suppressing testosterone without the use of an anti-androgen, which essentially rely on utilising oestrogen's natural ability to suppress testosterone when taken in high enough doses.

Honestly, the swiftness of changes really surprised me. Initially, the anti-androgen spikes your testoster-

one levels. It felt like being invited into a very loud and slightly chaotic room. Then after about four or five days, the HRT starts to kick in and all the chaos softens. It became a lot easier for me to function, I was no longer ruled by very direct and uncompromising thoughts, and slowly over the weeks and months following, I became a lot more in tune with my body and my emotional wellbeing. I could express myself and my thoughts with so much more kindness to myself and others.

Alongside my mental health drastically improving, my skin felt much more smooth, and some of my musculature started to change. My face became more rounded, my body became so much more femme, and it became easier to speak with much less bass in my voice. These improvements happened over several years, and I think HRT had reached its full effects for me after four years.

To Document or Not to Document?

I'm sure we've all seen those videos of people documenting their changes on hormones and vlogging their surgeries – I have, and I've also made plenty of my own!

It's become common and popular for trans people to document the changes they experience throughout their transitions, particularly on hormones, and it makes sense. Your voice changing, hair coming in or thinning out, body shape changing, face shape changing – *everything changing.* Whether you want to capture this on camera or not is a personal choice. If you do want to, don't feel

you have to share it online, or with anyone else. Honestly, when I first started posting videos on YouTube, I didn't expect anyone to watch them. It was mostly as a way to document things for myself.

Personally, I would recommend taking at least a couple of pictures and videos every so often throughout your journey. It wasn't the best feeling to take the 'before' photos, but I knew that I'd want to have them to look back on and remind myself of how far I'd come. You don't have to look back on them often (or ever), but it might be useful, and you can't rewind time to get them again.

Another reason to document things is because hormone changes are not overnight. I've seen a lot of people sharing frustrations online. They feel like they aren't experiencing changes, and they can get pretty down about it. The reality is probably quite different, as changes often occur but can be so gradual that we don't notice them day to day. Instead, it might take looking at photos and videos at three-to-six-month intervals to really notice how much your face shape or voice has changed. Documenting your journey can help you feel reassured that things are definitely progressing. If it's not your thing, though, you definitely don't have to do it.

Go in knowing what to expect when it comes to hormones, and pack a good amount of patience for your journey.

HRT can take time to be noticeable, but it's powerful, and totally worth the wait.

8

WHAT ABOUT 'THE SURGERY'?

H ave you had ... you know ... THE SURGERY?! *Dun ... dun ... duuuuunnnnnn* (cue dramatic zoom in on my very confused face).

When people ask this question, or refer to a 'sex change operation', they're referring to what is actually (colloquially) called 'bottom surgery' – surgery of the genital region – of which there is more than one procedure. Pretty much any trans person you talk to will have been asked this question at least once. Most probably (definitely) many more times than just once. I therefore wanted to kick this chapter off with a bit of myth-busting:

There is no such thing as 'THE SURGERY'.

Ask this question to a trans person and they won't even know how to answer it. 'The surgery? Which surgery? You need to be more specific.' Well, actually, you don't! It's not really the done thing to ask people about what surgery they've had.

There are many different surgical options available to trans people. These options depend on assigned sex at birth, transition stage, personal needs and outcomes, and they're not all in the genital region – despite the baffling fact that there's a good chunk of people who seem to be obsessed with what genitals you have if you're trans. Imagine asking every cis person you meet what their genitals look like. Strange.

Before we get into the different types of surgery, I need to put on my serious trans-dad hat for a second to share three important facts with you. Firstly, trans children never have surgeries. There are some people out there who like to sound the alarm and spread false information that literal children are going through various trans-related surgeries that they'll grow up to regret. This has never been the case, and it isn't happening now.

Secondly, you don't *need* to have surgery if you're trans. If it's not something you need to help with your dysphoria, or if it's not something you want to have, nobody should be forcing you to have surgery. Never feel pressured to do something that isn't right for you.

Finally, surgery *is* serious. In any form, surgery is strenuous on the body, and most transition-related surgeries are pretty major. Yes, it's something you're likely to be excited about, and yes, trans surgeries really can have a huge positive impact on your wellbeing – but they're still surgeries. It's important to research each specific surgery you want to have, go through pros and cons, and discuss potential options with your surgeon.

Surgery in general can – and does – go wrong sometimes. There's always the potential for mild or severe complications – trust me, I've been through them! Make sure you're fully aware of all of the risks before going ahead. There will also always be a recovery time, so make sure you've saved enough annual leave to recover sufficiently!

I also want to touch upon some important knowledge that I wish I'd had before my experiences with surgery, which applies to most of the procedures we talk about in this chapter:

- Results never look perfect straight away. Your body will need plenty of time to heal, which means it might take a while before you can enjoy and appreciate how you feel about your post-surgery self.

- Bruising can be intense, in colour, depth, size and feel. Don't push yourself too much during recovery. Post-surgery skin can feel *reeeeally* tight and very delicate. Listen to post-op care instructions to make sure you don't cause any accidental delays to recovery.

- Everyone is different, from healing, activity levels, pain and the appearance of results. Make sure you speak specifically to your surgeon about what to expect.

- Get on that post-op care and scar treatment as soon as you can to reduce redness and scar stretching.

- For bottom surgeries in particular: toilets and catheters are a *chore*. Beware of constipation (which is more common than you might think!) and take things slow.

Preparing for surgery and recovery

Plan ahead to have good support, both emotionally and physically!

Have realistic expectations.

Don't overestimate your physical ability.

Listen to your body.

Move common-use items to easily reachable places.

Write yourself a letter to read after surgery.

Know that anxiety is normal!

Ask all the questions you can.

WHAT ARE YOUR TOP TIPS FOR PREPARING FOR SURGERY AND RECOVERY?

'I'd advise people to be ready for possible post-surgery depression – I don't think it's talked about often enough. It doesn't mean you've made the wrong decision, but is simply your body being tired and stressed out, and that's totally okay.'

Peter, 29, trans man

As we've already said, any surgery is a pretty big deal. Not only should you be prepared, it's also super important that you take the pre- and post-care instructions seriously. The number one piece of advice I can give is to:

listen to your surgeon, and the medical staff involved in your post-operative care.

If they tell you to rest for a certain number of days, you rest for that number of days. If they tell you not to go to the gym for a couple of weeks, don't go to the gym for a couple of weeks. If they tell you to go up to every cute dog in the park and pet them, you go up to every cute dog in the park and pet them! (Seriously though: listen to advice about when and how dressings should and shouldn't be changed, and follow all the rules about antibiotics to a T - pun intended.)

As well as your surgeon, you need to listen to your

body. During recovery, don't push past what your body feels comfortable with doing, and definitely don't push yourself if both your body and your surgeon are saying not to! If something doesn't feel or look right, then get it checked out – most of the time you should be able to contact your surgeon and send them photos if you're worried something is wrong.

We're skipping ahead quite a bit here talking about recovery. Let's go over what various surgeries are available for trans people.

What Surgeries Are Available?

What I can cover in this chapter is only a segment of what your surgeon will detail to you during your consultations. It's important to do as much research as you can into any surgeries that you may be considering.

☆ **Top Tip:** *You're bound to have a load of questions – I sure did! Write them down on your phone whenever you think of them, and save them all up for your surgeon. Your consultation will feel less overwhelming, and you can be as informed and prepared as possible.*

So let's talk about what the different surgery options are. These are generally split two ways: by assigned birth sex, and by whether they happen to the top or the bottom of your body (top surgery and bottom surgery made simple!).

The reality is a lot more complex, and I've tried to lay this out visually for you before we go through the trans masc and trans femme surgeries in turn.

	trans masc	trans femme
Top surgery procedures	Double incision Periareolar (both fall under double mastectomy)	Breast augmentation
Bottom surgery procedures	Phalloplasty Metoidioplasty Potential extras: Scrotoplasty Urethral lengthening Vaginectomy Hysterectomy	Vaginoplasty Orchiectomy
Additional masculinisation/ feminisation procedures	Body masculinisation	Body feminisation Facial feminisation (rhinoplasty, chin or jaw augmentation, brow contouring, hairline lowering, hair transplant) Vocal surgery

Top Surgery trans masc

Generally speaking, this is where most breast tissue is removed from the chest (not all, but don't worry, even cis men have some), and nipples may be resized and positioned to look more typically masculine.

Double Incision	Periareolar
How? Bilateral scars are made along pec muscle line. Nipples are removed, resized and repositioned.	How? Small incisions are made around the nipples to remove breast tissue. Nipples are not removed and are typically not resized or repositioned.
Works better for fuller chests (B cup +)	Best for smaller chests (A cup −)
+ More consistent results with less chance of revision − More scarring − Recovery is typically longer	+ Less scarring − Higher chance of revision − Low flexibility for changing nipples

The choice in which top surgery you have will mostly come down to the size of your chest. Double incision is a more common procedure and works better for larger and fuller chests. Typically if you have a B cup or larger, this is what your surgeon will offer. Periareolar is less common, as it's typically best for chest sizes of A cups or smaller. Some (though very few) trans masculine people may not

WHAT ABOUT 'THE SURGERY'?

need top surgery for a flatter chest if they start with a very small chest or if they used puberty blockers.

I was technically within the criteria for periareolar, but as my chest was quite 'full', I wanted to minimise the risk of revisions. I also wanted my nipples to be smaller and repositioned, so double incision made the most sense for me.

I had top surgery in August 2012 and it was a combination of exciting and nerve-racking. It's still *surgery* after all, no matter how much it might change your life for the better. I had to arrive early on the day of my surgery and my mum came with me. My butt was hanging out of the awful paper underpants they gave me (true fashionista), and the surgeon marked up my chest.

☆ **Top Tip:** *If you're uncomfortable about having your chest marked up, you're not alone. It is necessary but very quick, and you should let your surgeon know about your discomfort so they can help you as best as they can.*

My surgery went very smoothly, and I woke up feeling a combination of relief, happiness, and like absolute shit (thanks, general aesthetic). I was given a post-op compression binder to aid healing, and could only walk around with my upper arms metaphorically glued to my sides like a T. rex for a couple of weeks. There were a couple of things I didn't expect about recovery. The *stink* was real, and baby wipes just didn't cut it after a while. Also, I hadn't expected to feel so ... flat? (Excuse the accidental pun.)

I was mentally happy to be post-op, but I was *so* physically uncomfortable. I was still in a binder, more than before actually, and I couldn't wash. The reveal also felt anticlimactic. My chest was bruised all over, my nipples looked like plastic caps, and the swelling raised my chest to a point where I was the same size as pre-surgery. I hate to sound ungrateful (and as soon as I had recovered I was elated!) but this feels important to share, because that magical reveal moment was ... not so magical for me, ha-ha. It's okay to feel this way.

The post-op binder disappeared after three weeks, the bruising after a month, and all the swelling after six months. I couldn't help but walk around the house shirtless a LOT. My dad would constantly tease me that my nipples would fall off. I still didn't wear a shirt.

I'm grateful for top surgery every day. It was the most drastic change to my life in terms of transitioning, and gave my dysphoria such a shove, I swear I could physically feel the relief.

WHAT'S IT LIKE TO GET PERIAREOLAR?

Anon. trans man, 25:

I was referred to public healthcare in 2017 and had periareolar two years later. My chest was small enough for peri, and as I live stealth, I wanted to avoid the larger scars from a double incision. I searched online for a surgeon whose results I liked and was really excited for a consultation. We briefly discussed double incision, but because I wanted peri and was in good shape, the surgeon was confident he could achieve the results I wanted and resize my nipples, and I had surgery a week later.

'Waking up from top surgery was the first time I'd felt anxious. I'd heard that sometimes excessive

breast tissue is left in, and I was super impatient to see my results and new nipples! I had a drain to prevent fluid build-up, dressings and a post-op binder to minimise swelling that I could have daily 20-minute breaks from. I went home the next day and felt surprisingly okay. I had to keep reminding myself to take it easy, which was difficult because I felt quite mobile.

'I took small peeks before my reveal a week later because I was anxious that I might need a revision. The reveal itself was underwhelming. I initially felt my chest didn't look that different from before surgery as it was so swollen, and it took a few months to see the proper results. Going back to the gym was a relief. I remember having a nip slip while working out and thinking I can't show that! But after mentally readjusting, it was a liberating feeling!

'I have a small bit of extra tissue, which bothered me for a while. I even had a revision booked, but the surgeon said it was a "don't fix what ain't broke" thing, which helped me feel confident enough (alongside my gym-going) to cancel the revision. I'm still a little hesitant to show my chest to people who don't know I'm trans, but I take every opportunity to be topless with people I'm comfortable around! Top surgery has exponentially reduced my overall dysphoria, and I have no chest dysphoria at all.

Some people can be quite elitist when they can get peri over double incision. I think it's important to remember that there's no 'better' surgery. There are differences, but some work better for some people, and others work better for others. The best results depend on what's right for you and your body.

Bottom Surgery trans masc

Generally speaking, this is when a penis and (sometimes) scrotum are created from existing genitalia or a skin graft. These are a lot more complex than top surgery, with longer recovery times and more variations available.

Phalloplasty (phallo)	Metoidioplasty (meta)
How? A skin graft from the forearm (most common), thigh or abdomen is used to create a phallus.	How? The testosterone-enlarged clitoris is reconfigured into a free-standing phallus.
Typically 3 stages	Typically 2 or 3 stages (depending on extras)
+ Average-sized penis is created + Penetrative sex is possible + Standing to pee is easier - Significant scarring, including on graft site - No natural erections, a pump system in the ball or semi-rigid rod can create erections instead - Higher risk of sensation loss - Skin colour and texture is less penis-like (though can be tattooed)	+ Natural erections + Less risk of sensation loss + Significantly less scarring + Natural colour and texture of genital skin - Results in micro-penis size - Penetrative sex is not always possible - Fly clearance when standing to pee is not guaranteed

Unlike top surgery where your body sort of dictates what procedure you have, it's totally up to your personal preference whether you get phallo or meta. Desired size typically heavily influences what trans masc people will go for. It's also worth noting that while top surgery feels crucial for a lot of trans masc people, bottom surgery may not be as important for reducing dysphoria.

Within each procedure, you can also opt for urethral lengthening (extending the urethra through your penis to allow you to pee standing up), scrotoplasty (creating a ball sac from the labia majora and implants), and a vaginectomy (removing the vagina and closing the vaginal opening). There's also the option of a hysterectomy (removing the reproductive organs). All of these extras may be done during stages of phallo or meta, or as stand-alone surgeries, but it's advised to get procedures done at the same time to reduce the number of operations (particularly urethral lengthening).

Meta felt right for me, as I didn't want a lot of scarring, and size wasn't as important to me as other factors such as feeling and sensation. Meta is more likely to retain feeling and sensation when compared to phallo, as it doesn't involve a skin graft, but instead involves reconfiguring elements that are already there.

I didn't feel like I needed bottom surgery to relieve my dysphoria until nearly five years after coming out. A big part of it was feeling mentally ready to have surgery again following top surgery, and it just took me that long for my dysphoria to impact me in a way that I needed to do something about it. I was referred on the public healthcare system in late 2015, and had two surgeries over a period of a year and a half.

My first stage of meta was in January 2018. T had already caused lower growth (of the clitoris), and this stage essentially releases it to be a free-standing phallus. I also had scrotoplasty, when my scrotum was made. It took me about eight weeks to recover from this, and I was given 'homework' to massage my scrotum in preparation for silicone testicular implants in the second stage – this is by far the most unusual homework I've ever been assigned! My second stage, in July 2019, simply involved inserting the implants (which sometimes needs to be done across two separate surgeries), and recovery for this was much simpler.

My first stage of meta is a reminder that things can go wrong during surgery. I have a great penis now, don't get me wrong ha-ha, but complications during procedures can always occur. In short, I had a haematoma from a caught artery, which required another surgery and a one-week hospital stay. It was a pretty difficult time, and led to a couple of very uncomfortable weeks of dressing changes, catheter usage, and waddling – though to be honest, these recovery elements are a given with any bottom surgery. Despite my experience, I don't regret any surgery I've had one bit. The psychological impact of bottom surgery was more positive than I thought it would be. It was like feeling complete, and finally belonging in my own skin. I could actually look at myself naked in the mirror – pretty cool.

I have to give a huge shout-out to my wife, Shaaba, who never left my side, slept on hospital chairs and floors, and supported me above and beyond. I don't know how I'd have coped without her.

Finlay Games is a 48-year-old trans man from the UK who has very kindly shared his phallo experience with us. You can read more about his journey in his memoir and personal guide, *Top to Bottom*.

FINLAY GAMES

I had phallo across six surgeries over three years; it's typically a three-stage surgery, but I had some complications that needed to be fixed. Top surgery was the biggest thing for me, but bottom surgery wasn't something I was sure I needed initially. I felt a societal pressure for the community: was I wanting surgery to prove my masculinity with a penis in some way, or did I need this surgery to work through my dysphoria? I was also put off by the lack of information and huge number of myths and misconceptions that surrounded lower surgery back then. I took my time to work through my thoughts and realised surgery was what I needed to feel comfortable. I also knew I wanted phallo, as standing to pee was important to me, and wasn't a guarantee with meta.

I underwent the first stage in August 2015. My penis was created from a skin graft taken from my forearm (skin from under my bum was then used to replace the skin taken from my arm), and they began creating my urethra. They also created a testicle so it would be fully healed for pump insertion at stage three, but surgeons don't often do this in advance anymore. Recovery from stage one was very difficult. I had 103 staples in my bum, my penis was in a bandage cage to keep it at a forty-five-degree angle to ensure blood flow and my arm was in a sling – you can't prepare for how immobilising that recovery is. After a year, I underwent stage two in April 2016, where they created the head of my penis, lengthened my urethra, did a vaginectomy, and I had a hysterectomy. I had my first test pee after ten days, and it was so liberating! I spent a week going round to different urinals where I was living at the time, ha-ha, it was just what I wanted!

Unfortunately, the joy of standing to pee was short-lived as at the first attempt of stage three, which involved fitting the erectile device, the surgeon discovered issues with my urethra. This delayed stage three from being carried out. After that, a severe infection also meant that my urethral hook-up had to be temporarily undone. My surgeon said urethral lengthening was like operating on a piece of wet spaghetti, so it's understandable why there are often complications from this stage. I finally healed and my urethra was hooked up again successfully. After this, I was at last able to have the erectile device fitted in August 2018, along with my second testicular implant.

The erectile device I have is inflatable, with a saline solution that goes between a reservoir in the abdomen and a cylinder in the penis, all controlled with a button in the testicle. Healing from this stage only took about ten days, and I had to wait six weeks before trying any self-pleasure or intercourse. It was odd feeling mechanical parts, getting used to how they work and understanding how a penis works. There's nothing to prepare you for how an erectile device will feel or function, and as trans men, we have no experience to draw on as to how to use a penis either. All of that played a part in the first few months of healing and getting used to the changes in my body.

The biggest impact wasn't the physical aspect of surgery, but the self-discovery I went through getting used to a penis and how it made me feel. I only found out I was gay because of the process I went through to know my body. My dysphoria shifted and I reached a really comfortable place of being – because of my penis, yes, but also because of the self-discovery it allowed me to have. When you can't enjoy your body, you don't really know who you are, and I personally needed a penis to do that. It wasn't the penis that made me a man, but it helped me be myself, which was everything.

It always feels uplifting talking to trans people, and I can relate a lot to the sense of completeness Finn describes, despite having had a very different surgery. Bottom surgery provided a sense of happiness in how my body looks now compared to before, but beyond that, it helped me *feel* better in every other way as well. The impact of bottom surgery isn't just the physical consequences of a surgical procedure, but part of a greater striving towards feeling comfortable and complete in yourself.

💜 **For the Allies:** *Learning about Finn's experience high-lights the difficulties of surgery and recovery. I can see many parallels in the toll this took on Jamie too, and also parallels in just how meaningful the results of surgery can be. It can be difficult to watch your loved* *one go through such intense surgical processes for things that may seem elective to you, and you may even feel a need to express this to them. It's important to be honest with your trans loved one, of course, and it's also important to remember in these conversations that these surgeries are not a choice for them, but a necessity to feel complete and at peace with themselves. – Shaaba*

Breast Augmentation trans femme

If oestrogen alone doesn't yield the desired results, trans femme people may want breast augmentation to further feminise their chest. If you're considering this, bear in mind that it can take multiple years for breasts to develop on hormones.

Breast augmentation

How? Implants are placed behind the breast tissue to improve breast fullness, shape and contours.

Consider the type of implant you get as it can affect your final results. Take your time at your consultation so that you can get the best idea of what you want.

+ Often consistent results
+ A lot of options for size
- You might not be able to sleep on your front as comfortably
- There will be some scarring

WHAT ABOUT 'THE SURGERY'?

Luxeria, a 33-year-old trans woman, shares her breast augmentation story:

It seems my body is quite receptive to the changes oestrogen provides, so I've been lucky with my chest growth from HRT alone. Four years into HRT I was a B cup and was quite happy with that size, but I definitely wanted my body to feel more feminine in a femme fatale sort of way. In 2022, I decided to undergo a breast enlargement.

I have a very specific image in mind for my personal style and wanted to reflect that with my choice of breast size, and there are SO many options! I wanted a modest increase in volume and size, while also sticking to my athletic build, and consultations with my doctor helped me decide the finer details that took me to a D cup with proportionate roundness.

As soon as I woke up after my surgery, I was so happy with the results. I had to wear a binder and a sports bra for eight weeks for compression and healing, which was an interesting feeling. It made my breasts feel slightly smaller at first, but now they've healed I'm so happy with them. My body feels in proportion, and my shape in clothes (and out of them) makes me feel so happy.

Vaginoplasty

Generally speaking, this is the removal of a penis and creation of a vagina, vulva and clitoris.

Vaginoplasty

How? The skin and nerves of the penis are used. The penis is inverted to create the inside of the vagina (if there's not enough penile skin, part of the sigmoid colon can be used), and the tip is used to create the clitoris. Regular dilation of the new vagina is required to prevent it from closing up.

+ Vaginal penetrative sex is typically possible
+ Can achieve good aesthetic results
+ Can typically still achieve orgasm
- Self-lubrication isn't always possible
- Orgasms may not be as intense
- Depth can be limiting during penetration

Veronica is a 37-year-old trans woman from Poland who now lives in the UK. She is a body piercer and works in a piercing studio, Pierce Me London, which prides itself in being a safe space for all LGBT+ identities.

VERONICA

I've been on hormones for many years, and I've had most, if not every trans-related surgery you could imagine. From multiple stages of facial feminisation, to breast augmentation, butt implants and vaginoplasty. I'd say I had two major surgeries each year for five years. I knew vaginoplasty was a surgery I needed to have as soon as I decided to be true to who I am.

I was sexually active before having surgery, but I didn't like how it felt to be fetishized for my genitals. I'm not shaming anyone else who might be in that position, it just never felt right for me personally. I didn't feel comfortable in myself having those parts, and practically, I also found it difficult to find clothes and underwear that I felt comfortable in.

I did a lot of research about vaginoplasty, and by the time I got the green light from the Gender Identity Clinic, I had saved up enough to pay for surgery myself and decided to go private for this. There were two reasons that influenced my decision: as I could afford it myself, I wanted someone else to have the NHS surgery place, and I also wanted the flexibility of choosing my own surgeon. After further research, I found a surgeon that I liked in Thailand and went there to have my surgery. I knew some people there, but the procedure and immediate recovery did feel quite lonely and physically intense, as I had gone on my own. I couldn't leave my bed for the first two weeks, and the stitches caused a lot of discomfort. One stitch in particular felt very painful, and the stitches on my clitoris were stiff and would catch on underwear.

Even after the pain from the stitches subsided, the rest of the recovery period was very intense. It took around six months before I could start enjoying the results, but I had to dilate three times a day for the first three months to stop the new vaginal opening from closing over. Over time, dilation got easier and needed to be done less frequently. I now only need to dilate once a week, and will need to do this for the rest of my life – but I have sex more frequently than that, so it's fine with me!

Now that I've had this surgery, I'm much more confident in myself. I find it easier to get clothes that I like, and I'm not at all shy to be naked. Vaginoplasty has verified a lot of things for me, has helped me to feel right sexually and has increased my levels of enjoyment more than I could imagine. There are differences and limitations that I'm aware of between my vagina and the vagina of a cis woman – things like depth and self-lubrication work differently – but this is my body and I love it. All of us women have different journeys and experiences with our bodies, whether we're cis or trans. I'm very at peace with mine.

If you are considering vaginoplasty, make sure that you are doing it for you, and not for anyone else.

Additional Procedures

While top surgery and bottom surgery are the most common, there are additional procedures that trans people may opt for. There's only really one for trans masc people, but quite a few for trans femme people, and all of them can greatly vary in how much they relieve someone's personal dysphoria.

- **Body masculinisation surgery (BMS)** is a type of surgical fat redistribution which moves fat reserves from one part of the body to another, or fully removes fat reserves, to create a more typically 'masculine' body shape for trans masc people.

- **Facial feminisation surgery (FFS)** is a series of surgeries, including rhinoplasty (to reconstruct the nose), jaw augmentation, brow contouring, shaving of the Adam's apple, hair transplant, lowering of the hairline, chin width reduction and more. The overall aim is to soften facial features, which is a typically feminine trait. All of these are optional, and some trans femme people feel changes in their face shape from HRT alone reduce their dysphoria.

- **Vocal surgery** alters the voice through various different procedures that range in invasiveness. It typically aims to reverse the lower voice caused by testosterone, and is often accompanied with vocal training. Trans femme people may just use vocal training, and not surgery, to reduce dysphoria.

- **Body feminisation surgery (BFS)** is a type of surgical fat redistribution that will either rearrange fat reserves or utilise implants to create a more typically 'feminine' body shape for trans femme people.

That's it for the surgical chapter. I know it was a major one with lots of info, and it can seem very overwhelming. Take your time, carry out extra research of your own, ask your surgeon all the questions you need to (if you're at that stage) and be as prepared as possible to recover fully.

9

DATING AND RELATIONSHIPS

You are lovable.

I don't think trans people get told this enough. I certainly didn't hear it – ever – when I first came out, and I think being told that I was lovable would have helped a huge amount. I did, however, realise this was a big concern for my mum. That somehow, coming out could change whether I would live a happy and fulfilled life, including finding a partner. Not because she didn't think I could or should, but because of society's opinion and treatment of trans people. So, to all the trans people reading who need to hear it: you *are* lovable.

Being trans doesn't exclude you from finding love in all of its forms.

This next chapter is all about your lovability as a trans person, and how to navigate dating and relationships.

I realise how weird it is to be talking about my mum at the beginning of a chapter all about dating, ha-ha, but there's just one more point I need to make. I've never told anyone this before, but I had the same worry she did, long before my mum shared hers. I didn't see happy, fulfilled, LOVED trans people anywhere. Whenever there was a trans person in the media, it was all about their misery, their 'sex change operation', the hate crime statistics. Nothing positive, nothing uplifting, no happy endings riding into the sunset. I also didn't see any trans people talking about dating, their relationships or finding love.

It's about ten years later, and I'm really glad there are now so many more positive and truthful trans stories, even if they do still focus heavily on the transitioning process. That's why Shaaba and I started vlogging. All of the trans guys I used to watch on YouTube stopped making videos when they hit one year on T or had top surgery. No one should feel forced to continue making content, of course, but it felt a bit weird. Almost lonely. The representation seemed to disappear, and with it, so did my glimpse of what life as a trans person could look like beyond medical transitioning milestones. What about relationships, and life away from being trans?

I went so far in believing that being trans excluded me from love that I genuinely thought that my only way to experience dating and relationships was to delay coming out and transitioning. I was 16 at the time, I identified as a lesbian, and had been in two relationships so far, neither of which had felt right because *I* didn't feel right. They also ... just ... weren't right. I really wanted to experience those 'typical' teenage moments of dating. Flirting, going on a cringey date, having that 'do they/don't they like me' panic. But I just couldn't hold off being myself.

This is all sounding really sad, but I'm pleased to report that none of my fears were true. I've been in a relationship for the past 11 years with someone who loves me and accepts me fully for who I am. That sounds like such a flex, but I don't mean it to be. That's personally what *I* was looking for in terms of love. I've never wanted to be a serial dater, but lots of people *love* casual dating and flings, and that's absolutely being successful in love too.

Let's do some quick stats. Of the five closer friends that I have who are trans, and the 14 other trans people I can think of more distantly (I gave myself 30 seconds to write a list), 17 out of those 19 have had success in dating and relationships. Many of them are in long-term relationships now, most have had long-term relationships, and all except one successfully date.

Pre-warning: my personal experience does mean that I have little experience of dating as a trans person, and absolutely zilch experience of using dating apps. Shaaba knew me before I came out, so I've never had to come out to someone in a romantic or dating context either. But don't fear: this chapter is still going to be packed with lots of super-useful advice about dating as a trans person, with plenty of other trans voices helping me!

Entering the World of Dating

I want to clarify *which* world of dating we're entering into. This isn't a section on dating generally, but specifically on dating as a trans person (and a little bit about dating *a* trans person too). This actually makes things a little simpler for me, because dating and trans dating are not worlds apart! There's definitely a misunderstanding among both cis and trans people, that dating becomes something entirely different when someone is trans. We're not aliens, we just have a slightly different lived experience that doesn't necessarily *have* to impact dating and relationships in a big way.

The way trans people find dating and relationship partners, for example, is much the same as for cis people. I found my partner in college. Maybe you're into someone from your school, or university, or workplace. Of course, we can't forget that a lot of modern-day happily-ever-after stories begin on dating apps, the concept of which terrifies me. Not because I'm trans, but because I'm genuinely so awful at flirting. You should hear me with Shaaba – if we weren't already in love I'm sure I'd be single.

As a trans person, how did you meet your current partner?

Through friends   At university

At an anime convention

At a trans group   On a dating app

At church   At school

At work   At a house party

Dating Apps

Dating apps are so varied. Many mainstream ones allow you to share that you're trans publicly on your profile, if that's something you want to do. For apps that don't have this as a feature, some trans people choose to share this anyway in their bios. Some apps have the aim of being trans-friendly and inclusive – but do keep in mind that this doesn't mean every individual using the app will be trans-inclusive, even if the company has this ethos. It's definitely a good idea to shop around and find which apps you feel most comfortable using.

There are dating apps made specifically for the LGBT+ community, and some, even more specifically, for trans people. Some trans people feel most comfortable dating other trans people, or happen to socialise with other trans people more frequently, leading to 'T4T' (or 'trans for trans') relationships. It's perfectly okay for people to want T4T relationships. It makes sense that a shared experience, unspoken understanding, and guaranteed acceptance of your identity would take away some of the scary aspects of dating.

What's *not* okay is that trans people should only ever be expected to date other trans people. I've been told by multiple people that it would just 'make sense' for me to date not only a trans person, but an 'opposite trans person'. The idea behind these suggestions comes from cishet-normative expectations of traditional sex posi-tions and having biological children. But people are not two parts of a puzzle that must fit together in a very traditional way – not to mention, not all trans people are straight. Segregating marginalised groups and expecting them to only find love with each other is at best an unnecessary limitation, and at worst discriminatory.

Regardless of which apps you're using, we all know how important it is to stay safe when it comes to online dating. For trans people there are a couple of extra safety considerations to keep in mind. Everybody has to kiss a few frogs, and sometimes those frogs can turn out to be particularly toxic if they don't take the news of you being trans very well. This might not even be in person, so think carefully before you trust someone with personal information and photos (including those naughty nudes). You wouldn't want those being shared without your permission, or used to out you in wider contexts.

If you are meeting in person, please make sure that you tell a trusted person in your life who you are meeting and where. This should be a general dating rule but is especially important if you plan on coming out on that particular date, just in case you've found a toxic frog.

Alex Woolhouse is a 27-year-old trans woman from the UK. She's been on at least 500 dates so far, and has a lot of experience to share! Alex also has an incredible podcast, *How Not to Get a Boyfriend*, where she talks about being trans, looking for love and navigating dating.

ALEX WOODHOUSE

So much discussion about transness is focused on transitioning and rights, which are super important, but there's less on what life is actually like if you're trans. Looking for love is universal, so I wanted to discuss the similarities (and also the differences) of how every girl is dating in London. I am looking for love, but whoever is going to stop my amazing single life needs to be the right guy, not just someone for the sake of being in a relationship. I go into every date thinking they could be my husband, but I also enjoy the fun and flirty nature of being fancied by someone cute. It's fun! It's also something I feel I have to do. As a straight trans woman, I don't have time for it to suddenly become non-stigmatised to have a trans girlfriend, so I have to be part of the conversation that normalises it.

I use dating apps, and mostly don't share that I'm trans on my profile. It's definitely easier when I do, because then I can talk about all the everyday things people talk about, and part of that, for me, is my transness. I don't have to think, Oh no, I can't say that in case I inadvertently microdose that I'm trans on a date. I used to tell all my dates before I met them, which often meant I wasn't getting to actual dates. I thought to myself that I wished I could get a chance, not to prove myself, but to show that dating a trans woman is completely normal. That's what the vast majority of my dates say: that they've not dated a trans girl before, and that the date has been lovely. I know that it has nothing to do with my transness, and it hasn't been a barrier. I feel I have to get to a point where I trust that a guy will treat me like a human being once he knows. I used to think I was going into dates with a huge secret that a date had to be okay with, but actually, my comfort in sharing my identity is something my date has to earn.

It's 50/50 on whether my transness is important to my dates, and there are so many who don't care. They'll say they're attracted to me, that it isn't something they've thought about before, and that they're happy to continue the date, or whatever the interaction is. The other half will thank me for telling them and say it's not really something for them. That's fine, and it actually doesn't have anything to do with me. They've seen me, they've fancied me, they've swiped right on my profile, they've bought me a glass of Sauvignon Blanc! I think about their life experience so far, be that in sex, relationships, porn even. How does that make them respond to the knowledge that the girl they're dating is trans? It becomes a much less personal thing, because it's up to them, and it's on them.

For a while, that rejection felt like it was all about me. It takes a while to uncouple that, but there's nothing for you to be apologetic about. Being trans is not undesirable, it's not weird. It's completely normal, and it's up to them how they square that. This is a part of modern dating. Some girls might be trans, or bi, or disabled, or working class – all of these different things. I would say any guy who dates girls, and is attracted to girls, has the capacity to be attracted to trans women. Trans is just another descriptor and a different type of woman, and there are loads of different types. This way, they can reject me for being mouthy, or for having a podcast – and that's completely fair enough!

Every time I go on a date and there's an absolute hunk of a man in front of me, and he's laughing at all of my jokes and listening to every word I say, I think back to 14-year-old me. At that age, all I wanted was for one of the boys on the school rugby team to fancy me. If she could see me now, she'd be so excited and impressed. I wish I could tell her that it was okay, and that she'd be a hot blonde girl with nice boobs, dating all the hunks. I'd tell her that boys will fancy her – which feels like the most important thing in the entire world at that age – and I'd tell her that it's going to happen for her, because for so long, it felt like it wouldn't.

☆ **Top Tip:** *Alex's initial fear of rejection is something I see so many trans people relate to, myself included. Framing my transness as the descriptor that it is helped me, and it could help you too. There are so many things about everybody that someone might not like, or might not want to date somebody for. So be safe, but know that your transness isn't a reason to prevent you from living your best dating life.*

Alex again:

Safety is important, and cis straight guys can be quite a worrying demographic. I'm more aware of the risks of dating as a woman, compared to dating as a gay man. Late-night hook-ups are so normalised in the gay dating scene, but the risk increases as a trans woman with a cis guy. I know I'm very privileged to be out, but there are still things that I do to reduce risks: always having Find My Friends on, texting a screenshot of my date's profile to my friends, making sure my phone is charged, organising a ride home, things like that. These are all things that every girl I know does as well, cis or trans. I don't subscribe to the idea that trans people shouldn't do certain things because they're inherently in a more vulnerable position. We know that, but you can do things that mitigate that risk, while knowing that you deserve love.

💜 **For the Allies:** *As a cis woman, I find Alex's amazing dating journey enlightening as well as fun. Cis men have always been a concern for women's safety, but speaking with Alex made me realise how little difference there is between cis and trans women dating. I don't say this to trivialise trans journeys – harrowing statistics reflect that trans women are disproportionately harmed, and society often places extra responsibility on trans women to protect their identities. At the same time, I could relate to most of Alex's steps of staying safe as a dating woman, because trans women are women. Some cis men may use transness as an excuse to behave violently, but all women carry concern of violence. Alex shared that dating is one of the greatest common factors and points of relatability among women, from requiring similar support to sharing similarly funny stories over brunch. I couldn't agree more. – Shaaba*

> **WHAT'S YOUR BEST ADVICE FOR STAYING SAFE WHILE DATING AS A TRANS PERSON?**
>
> 'Always meet someone new in public.'
>
> *Charlie, 28, woman (trans woman/intersex)*
>
> 'Stay open about what you want and what you are comfortable with, and make sure that the person is accepting before going deeper in the relationship.'
>
> *Louis, 24, trans man*
>
> 'Know when to block, delete and move on! I would recommend meeting up for a coffee or a meal first to understand what vibes they give off, and trust your gut if you want to bring a guy back to your house.'
>
> *Jonathan, 30, trans man*

When Do I Tell Them?

A big question that comes up around being trans and dating is when to tell someone you're trans. The answer to this largely depends on when you feel comfortable and safe, and while there's no magical formula that spits out a date, there are two guiding factors to help you determine the big 'when'.

The primary factor, and it's one that must be taken seriously, is consent around sex. Not only is it the right thing to do (and hey, consent is totally hot), it's also the legal thing you have to do. For example, potential partner(s) need to be fully aware if you're going to use a pack-and-play device, and so naturally, coming out would need to happen before this.

The second factor is when you determine a potential partner *should* know. I know, I know: *Jamie, you cop out.* This feels very non-specific, but that's because there are so many differences that influence when this could be. Maybe you're the kind of person who's very upfront; you might have it in your bio, or told people before a first date, because that's just a rule you want to live by. Maybe you've had a not-so-great past experience that's led you to be more cautious now. If telling a previous date resulted in them publicly and abruptly ending things, it would make sense why somebody might now choose to go on a first date and only decide to tell them once they're sure they wanted to see them again (they might even decide to not come out in person this time).

It could be that you go on a date, have a whirlwind romance, and get all the butterflies super fast so you want to tell them because it's getting serious. Or maybe you're taking things super slow. If you've only gone on three dates in three months, it might take you longer to feel ready to come out to someone.

The attitude of the person you're dating might impact when you come out to them. Maybe they brought up how awesome they think Elliot Page is, and now you know, *this is your moment.* Or maybe they say something that's a huge red flag and instead of coming out of the closet, you climb out the bathroom window (can you tell I've watched too many rom-coms?).

See? So many influences. The biggest one definitely

seems to be personality. Some people don't want to potentially waste their time developing a connection unless they know that person is accepting, while others want to know if they're going to develop a connection before being so open about their transness. I personally would opt to have my transness front and centre so that I wouldn't have to come out in person, and so I'd avoid spending time with someone who might not want to continue dating after finding out I'm trans. Again, there's no right or wrong answer.

WHY DID YOU COME OUT TO YOUR PARTNER WHEN YOU DID?

'My partner is a cis woman. I came out when it got to a point where I couldn't hide who I was. I needed to tell them for my own wellbeing.'

Eve, 26, trans woman

'I've been with my partner since November 2018, and we met on Tinder. We live together now, and he's a cisgender gay man. I was always open in all my dating profiles about being trans. As a queer man, usually when you chat to other men there's an expectation to share pictures prior to hooking up, so being open just weeds out the guys who aren't interested in having sex with (or dating) a trans guy. It doesn't bother me – I transitioned in 2008, so once you've dealt with everything that being trans entails for ten years you become thick-skinned!'

Jonathan, 30, trans man

'My partner is cis and bisexual. We both came out as bi to one another before we were even dating, I think. It was a huge 'nothing' thing for us. I came out to him the same time I came out to myself, in the same loud exclamation.'

Anon., 37, non-binary/trans masc

Would You Date a Trans Person?

This next section is for trans people, and some ♥ for the allies too. People seem pretty obsessed with genitals when it comes to trans people, and there's no situation where this is more obvious than dating. It's not uncommon to hear people say that they won't date a trans person, and sometimes this is because they're only thinking about what's between your legs. It's important not to assume anyone's genitals, cis or trans. You don't know what anybody might be sporting unless they tell you (and it's a bit of a weird conversation starter for a first date if you ask me!).

Putting genitals to one side (figuratively of course), cis people declaring whether they'd date a trans person or not has become a matter of hot debate. We know the world has been built in a very normative way. Not just for cis and straight people, but for able bodies, and white people, and men and so on. Stating preferences when it comes to dating, particularly when they're about marginalised groups, is more widely recognised now as being damaging. As it should be, because often these preferences come from a place of unconscious bias that tells us what we should find attractive, and it's what society deems to be 'normal'.

I want to make a couple of things clear. Firstly, no person, trans or cis, should *have* to date anybody. At the same time, claiming, unprompted, that you would never date any trans person is transphobic. Both things can be true. It's also very different from having a preference for how you have sex. For example, someone might not want to sleep with anybody who has a penis, and that's perfectly okay; but that's different to saying that you date women, but you'd never date a trans woman. That's not okay. The transphobic aspect often comes in because the people who state they'd never date trans people as a blanket rule don't see trans people as their true gender (as in, they don't see trans women as women, or trans men as men).

Which leads me to my second clarification: dating (or even fancying) trans people doesn't change your sexuality. Trans people are not magical sexuality switch flickers. The term 'trans' is just a prefix, and an adjective. Just like being tall, or brunette, or sporty can describe who you are. So if you're a straight cis man who finds a trans woman attractive, it doesn't change the fact that you're straight (just as finding brunettes attractive wouldn't change your sexuality either).

Sometimes those around you might try and dispute this. Straight cis men might get teased for being gay, which is not just transphobic, but also homophobic, as the term 'gay' here is used inauthentically and in a demeaning way. Sometimes people within the LGBT+ community themselves might dispute this (though it's quite uncommon). For example, cis people dating trans people might be challenged on why they don't identify as bisexual, or pansexual. This is an inauthentic portrayal of those sexualities, and again transphobic, as it stems from not seeing trans people as their true gender.

On the complete flip side, there are some cis people who exclusively seek out the experience of sleeping with, or dating, trans people just because they're trans. This is known as a fetish. I'm not here to tell anybody, including trans people, how to experience their attractions. There's nothing wrong with just wanting to be with someone for sex, and if everyone involved is upfront, open, consenting and comfortable with the situation, then that's all good. Make sure that you're comfortable with what you're doing, and who you are doing it with. It's important to be aware that there are people out there who objectify trans people, particularly trans women. You're not just there to fulfil someone's curiosity.

> There are plenty of people, trans and cis, who will happily date a trans person, not because you're trans, or despite you being trans, but because they like you for you.

That's what you deserve.

In Reverse

So far, we've covered a lot about when to tell someone

you're trans as you're entering a new dating situation. But what if you're already in a relationship when you realise you're trans? Lots of people discover their gender identity when they're already married, or in long-term relationships.

Coming out to a partner is often difficult for everyone involved and can lead to the unwanted ending of a relationship. If your gender identity is the opposite to how you've been previously presenting, it may now conflict with your partner's sexuality. The same goes for if your sexuality changes.

Nobody is to blame when this happens.

There's a fantastic book called *Some Body to Love* by Alexandra Heminsley that's a brilliant read generally, but especially if you're in a similar situation. There are situations where relationships still work after someone comes out as trans.

Ultimately, you deserve to be your true self, and find love as your true self.

Dysphoria and Sex

We've already dedicated a whole chapter to dysphoria, but I thought this context deserved its own little section. The beast is tricky to navigate at the best of times, and the intimacy of sex and dating can make it a little trickier still.

I found dysphoria particularly tricky during intimacy, because it wasn't just me that could see my body. I didn't know what would necessarily trigger my dysphoria, and I didn't know how to communicate when I was feeling particularly dysphoric to my partner.

Aside from transitioning to reduce my dysphoria, what helped was exploring what I was and wasn't comfortable with in terms of terminology, activities and boundaries. What *really* helped was then talking openly with my partner about this. People should always be open to discussing boundaries, and boundaries should always be respected within any context of intimacy.

These boundaries might change over time as you transition, and so might your dysphoria and triggers. Honesty is always the best policy, and it's important to keep communicating with intimate partners as this happens. Some of the most valuable lessons I learnt were to share with Shaaba what terminology I liked being used in reference to my body, to have a codeword that signalled that the dysphoria flag was waving, and to take things slowly to begin with if I was feeling unsure.

Never do anything that you're uncomfortable with, or that you don't want to do.

HOW DID YOU DEAL WITH DYSPHORIA DURING INTIMACY, DATING AND RELATIONSHIPS?

'It's such a two-way street. The trans person should not be the only one having to set boundaries and have to start conversations about intimacy. It is so important to have a partner who is patient and listens, and to offer them the same courtesy. Everyone has boundaries when it comes to intimacy and I found that so helpful to remember, because I have often felt like a burden or a problem.

'A big one I found is my girlfriend's surprise at how many things *weren't* a hard no for me as a trans person. And I also had to realise myself that when I am with someone who I know completely sees me as me, that some things that I would have expected to have been a hard no are actually fine with the right person. And that doesn't undermine my transness, and doesn't mean my dysphoria isn't real.'

Jamie, 20, trans man

'Lots and lots of communication. Before getting intimate I always make sure dysphoria triggers have been discussed, and we check in to make sure everyone is feeling good as things progress.'

Matt, 26, trans femme enby

'I try to be upfront about what my body can/can't do and communicate when things come up to adjust as needed, or stop.'

Sanjay, 30, transgender man

From Dating to Relationships

Going from dating to being in a relationship is always a rollercoaster, regardless of whether you're trans or cis. People often think that the fact I'm trans must be such a hindrance to Shaaba, and that it comes up in every minute of us being together. Truth be told, we both often forget that I'm trans. In fact, when writing this chapter, I asked Shaaba, 'Do you think you'd date someone who was trans?' Ha-ha-ha-ha.

💜 **For the Allies:** *It's true! While supporting Jamie at the beginning of his transition, his transness had a very frequent presence in our relationship. We were learning how to navigate each other's boundaries, and Jamie's specific changes – not to mention we were both generally growing into ourselves too. Over time, though, it's become something we literally only talk about when we want to. If we didn't do so much LGBT+ activism, it would rarely come up in our conversations. The only times we really talk about Jamie's transness in a personal context is at Trans Pride events (which are great fun!), and when family planning. Know that conversations won't always be taken up with T+ topics, even if it might feel that way at the beginning. – Shaaba*

I can only think of three aspects of being in a relationship that are affected by being trans. The first we've covered in quite a bit of depth already, and that's dealing with the people who now enter your life because of the relationship that you're in. Shaaba's family had a big impact on my transness and vice versa, and that's always a consideration when you enter a new relationship. Not to influence the direction or success of a relationship, but to make sure you can both be on the same page with how to approach potential non-acceptance from wider networks.

The other two aspects that could be affected by transness are optional steps in relationships: marriage and having children. Marriage isn't a hugely common occurrence, or a 'norm' in LGBT+ communities, as it is in most cishet communities. It's because access to marriage for LGBT+ people did, and still does, require fighting for. Gay marriage, for example, is still not accepted worldwide, and as a trans person in the UK, I could only marry as a man once I had my Gender Recognition Certificate (GRC). This can be a lengthy and costly process, and it isn't guaranteed (we'll speak more about this later), but I wanted to highlight that when we were planning our wedding this was an extra hoop we had to jump through because I was trans. Shaaba and I got married in September 2022, and personally, getting a GRC was totally worth it to have such a magical weekend of celebrations! I got to marry my best friend as my true self, in a safe space with lots of loved ones, and it was full of laughter, pride and lots of cake. Perfection!

In terms of having children, being trans has self-explanatory impacts, but in some ways can be seen as no different to cis people who are naturally infertile for a variety of health reasons. Being trans may not just affect your ability to have biological kids traditionally, but family-making in other ways too. For example, public healthcare services (like the NHS in the UK) require straight couples to try conceiving naturally for at least two years before they can access services like IVF. Well, I hate to pop the government's regulation bubble on this one, but no matter how long we try to conceive for, I think we might be a loophole to this rule! It can then be a bit of a postcode lottery as to whether public health services will help with your family-building efforts, as it is for cis same-gender couples too.

These are just some extra considerations to keep in mind – but none of them make you any less of a partner, or potential parent. Whether you're a happily single pringle, searching for sexy fun times, looking for love, or in a committed relationship, your transness doesn't stop you from finding happiness.

10

NAVIGATING A BINARY WORLD WHEN YOU'RE … WELL, NOT

'Non-binary people have always existed
– and always will.'

Shiv, 27, non-binary

I've tried to be inclusive throughout this book, but I want to dedicate some time to specifically provide information for non-binary people, and for non-binary voices.

Many people are non-binary. If you can fit into the binary of being either a man or a woman, you can also fit outside of these. Venn diagrams aren't limited to the circles, they include the spaces between and around the circles too. People aren't just straight or gay, people can be bi, for example (considered somewhere in between), or ace (considered outside of the binary attraction) as well. A million shades exist between black and white, and many things that we consider to be binary are actually a spectrum. Some people feel they fit somewhere in between the two binaries, and some people are absolutely nowhere to be found on that scale. There's no right or wrong way to be non-binary.

The existence of non-binary identities, and more than two genders, has been recognised across many different cultures for a hell of a long time, which is why it's the biggest pile of rubbish when you hear people prattle on about non-binary people being some kind of 'new-fangled fad'.

Welcome back Shiv, the 27-year-old journalist, broadcaster and physicist who is non-binary, who we heard from about intersectionality back in Chapter 2.

SHIV

Non-binary people have always existed – and always will. The same goes for trans and gender-diverse people. Oppressive gender norms have come out of a capitalist patriarchy and religious ideology. In ancient India, where my family is from, there is a long history of Hijras, enuchs, Kothis, Aravanis, Jogappas or Shiv-Shakthis, who are groups or tribes of transgender and/or intersex people. Ancient India would have also included countries such as Bangladesh and Pakistan, which gained independence after the British colonial rule.

Some people within these communities were revered and considered closer to God. There are even ancient texts that make distinctions between physical sex and psychological sex, which is what we might call gender identity in today's language. These positive attitudes towards trans, non-binary, gender non-conforming and intersex people are therefore not new. Indigenous cultures in regions all around the world have accepted a 'third gender' for centuries, from Oaxaca State in Mexico, to native North American tribes, to Samoa and Madagascar.

You Don't Owe Androgyny

Non-binary people do not owe anyone androgynous presentation to be valid or accepted as non-binary. Binary men and women (both trans and cis) are under no requirement to express themselves in a way conforming to their gender, and non-binary people aren't either.

Many non-binary people feel a pressure to present androgynously, or to present in a way that shifts against the stereotypes expected from their assigned sex at birth (so whether they are AMAB or AFAB).

Your identity isn't dependent on your expression.

This is true for non-binary people too!

Gendered Spaces

These are tricky for trans people generally, but particularly for non-binary people. Have a think about all the public spaces that exist: toilets, changing rooms, sports teams, prisons, refuges – basically anything in the world that is typically gendered. In most scenarios, there isn't a non-gendered option for non-binary people, with the exception of the rare gender-neutral toilet, or mixed sports team. This can be particularly uncomfortable to navigate for non-binary people.

HOW DO YOU NAVIGATE GENDERED SPACES?

'Toilets are hard. If I'm presenting in what could be considered a more "femme" way, I tend to just use women's toilets, but if I'm more "andro", I tend to decide based on safety, comfort or availability of what I can access.'

Matt, 26, trans femme enby

'I try to avoid gendered bathrooms, but I spend a lot of time on a college campus, so sometimes it can't be avoided. There are some gender-neutral bathrooms (which is great), but they're generally single-stall and are also disabled bathrooms so they're often occupied. I'm not worried about someone thinking I'm in the wrong bathroom, but I don't like how I feel. There's some shame attached somehow, like it's my fault for causing this situation I'm in (logically, of course it's not).'

Jess, 25, non-binary

'I usually only go to places where I feel comfortable, and it just so happens that many of these places have gender-neutral/-free facilities. If I'm caught in a place, bursting for a wee where there are only gendered options, I would usually go first to the 'ladies" bathroom. This is for a couple of reasons: I'm still often mistaken for a woman, so if someone was to 'create trouble', I feel that would be less likely to happen in those spaces. I also have no use for a urinal, and a ladies'' toilet would usually have more cubicle options. Having to extensively think about where I would pee is exhausting; gender-free spaces can be more inclusive and offer greater privacy for people of any gender.'

Shiv, 27, non-binary

The Legal Bits of Being Non-Binary

As with the social lack of inclusion through a lot of very gendered spaces, there's also a great lack of legal recognition and protections for non-binary people. In the UK, non-binary people aren't explicitly covered under the current Gender Recognition Act, and recent calls to have this changed to be more inclusive have been rejected. This means that non-binary people are not able to legally be recognised as non-binary, including on things such as passports where an 'F' or 'M' gender marker must be shown. Updating passports to include an 'X' gender-neutral marker has been rejected as recently as mid-2021. In more positive news, what *is* available is the usage of 'Mx', an accepted gender-neutral title in the UK. It's not enough, but it's a start.

Other countries around the world have made promising progress.

Countries including Austria, Belgium, Canada and several

more offer at least *some* legal recognition of non-binary identity. These recognitions range from the removal of gender on ID cards, and allowing X gender markers on official documentation.

SHIV

Currently there is no legal recognition for non-binary people in the UK, and I would love for this to change. It probably wouldn't massively change my day-to-day life, but it would change those big moments. If I ever got married, I would be addressed correctly rather than as 'wife'. Or if I ever have children, I would legally be 'parent' rather than 'mother' or 'father'. Perhaps the biggest one is being legally recognised as who I am when I die.

I would love all of that to be the case for me, but I'm ashamed to say that if I was given the opportunity to have my non-binary identity recognised in UK law, I probably wouldn't take it up, not right now at least. The world we live in is still so hostile to trans, non-binary and gender-diverse people, and the risk of facing prejudice feels too high when handing my ID to an ignorant person – whether that's at border control, or at a supermarket trying to buy pre-mixed cocktails! Allowing people to change their gender markers would just be step one in fully recognising non-binary identities legally. To really celebrate legal recognition of non-binary people, the process would have to be accessible, financially and mentally.

A legal change would no doubt see a shift in social attitudes too. A country like the UK recognising these identities could also create more acceptance on a global stage. That would be brilliant, but gender identities aren't really anything to do with the people around you; they are inherently personal. Having legal recognition would ultimately allow non-binary people to live and die with dignity.

Transitioning

Non-binary people *can* medically transition. Many non-binary people take hormones, and even have surgeries. Many don't, and neither option is right or wrong. Non-binary people have as much right and need to access gender-affirming healthcare as binary trans people do.

AS A NON-BINARY PERSON, HAVE YOU TAKEN HORMONES OR UNDERGONE ANY SURGICAL PROCEDURES?

'I'd love the deeper voice and the muscle gain and the fat redistribution, but there are other parts of my body that would change that currently I like how they are, so for now, I'm not pursuing any hormonal changes. I don't feel any less non-binary, because there are so many ways to be non-binary. Everyone's relationship to their body and their gender is different.'

Jess, 25, non-binary

'I've been on testosterone for two and a half years, and got top surgery three days ago. Many people assume that because of this I'm a trans man, and non-binary was just a stepping stone. Actually, these were to make me feel more like me, and don't mean that I'm a trans man after all. I don't regret either step of medically transitioning. It feels so good to be in a body where I can actually look at myself in the mirror and feel good. I would love to have a look that makes everyone question my gender, but most of all I just want to feel confident and comfortable in my own body.'

Asher, 23, AFAB non-binary

'I recently had top surgery, which was a huge step towards affirming my gender. My chest was something I was uncomfortable with from pretty much the time I started puberty, and before I knew what "trans" or "non-binary" meant at age 12, I was already binding my chest — I didn't even know the word "binding" either. Accessing top surgery was hard. It wasn't covered by the NHS, and I found that not all private clinics perform top surgery on non-binary patients. It was a long process of saving, researching and being on waiting lists.

Surgery itself felt like the biggest thing in the world to me, but I was worried about how people might respond. It turns out that everyone around me is happy and supportive. They say they can see a change in how happy I am and how confident I am with my body. So far, it's the only medical gender affirmation I've had, and I think it's all I will have. It's what is right for me.'

Shiv, 27, non-binary

11

WHO YOU GONNA CALL? MYTH-BUSTERS!

'Back off, man. I'm a scientist.'

Dr Venkman, Ghostbusters

O h yes, it's time for some myth-busting. Like ghost-busting but more annoying, especially when it comes to transphobes.

We've dabbled in busting myths throughout the book, but in this chapter we'll be going over some of the biggest and most frequent myths used to try and harm the trans community. Often presented as half-truths, I want to unpack some of these for you, provide you with some optional further reading to explore facts and hopefully give you a resource to pass on to others who might not be fully informed about trans issues, despite talking about it a lot.

Ready? Let's go, myth-busters!

Myth: Trans people are not the gender they say they are.

Wrong. This simply isn't true, but that doesn't stop an unfortunate group of transphobic people from disrespecting trans identities, stating trans people will always be their assigned sex at birth. They refer to trans women as men, trans men as women, and non-binary people as women or men, and of course use the wrong pronouns in all these contexts.

Trans women are women. Trans men are men. Non-binary people are non-binary.

Trans people living our lives doesn't cause harm to anybody, but deliberately disrespecting and misgendering trans people does cause harm.

💜 **For the Allies:** *You don't need to understand or even accept trans people to be respectful. The same goes for all marginalised groups, or people who are different to you.* – Shaaba

Myth: XX chromosomes make you a woman, XY chromosomes make you a man.

Wrong. People with this viewpoint label others as a woman or a man based only on something that can't be seen: one's chromosomes. They assume all trans men have XX chromosomes and must therefore be women, and that all trans women have XY chromosomes and must therefore be men.

The truth is a majority of people don't even know what their chromosomes are (and won't unless they take a DNA test). There are more chromosomal combinations than XX and XY, and many people – cis and trans women and men – don't have XX or XY chromosomes.

Not only does this myth conflate sex and gender, which are two separate things, it also reduces sex down to only chromosomes, ignoring three other dimensions of sex: primary sex characteristics, secondary sex characteristics and legal sex. Primary sex characteristics are the characteristics we're born with that are typically sex-characterised: genitals and reproductive organs. Secondary sex characteristics are physical attributes that typically occur at puberty, including breasts and facial hair.

Trans people can (and often do) change their primary and secondary sex characteristics through medically transitioning, and many countries allow trans people to change their legal sex marker too. Changing these things does not make trans people 'more trans' or 'more their gender'. The ability to change these things, however, means that transphobes who assume they can tell who has XX and XY chromosomes, and claim that chromosomes are the only determining factor of sex, are very mistaken!

Myth: TERFs/gender-critical transphobes are logical and just want to protect women.

Wrong. Trans-exclusionary radical feminists (or TERFs), who sometimes use the term 'gender-criticals' (or GCs), are transphobes who try to justify their transphobia under the guise of protecting women. Not all TERFs or GCs recognise that they're being transphobic, but still cause harm to the trans community. Further, the transphobic efforts of TERFs and GCs can also indirectly harm all women too, including cis women. This can happen because the frequent fixations of linking gender to genitalia (e.g. saying that 'all women have boobs, vaginas and periods, not penises') reduce women to their body parts, which is something feminists have been fighting against for decades. Not to mention it can ostracise cis women too (e.g. women post-menopause, women who have had breast removal or hysterectomies due to cancers, and so on).

Additionally, the constant linking of gender expression traits to gender identity can negatively affect all women, including cis women (for example, encouraging other transphobes to identify and publicly shame trans women based on physical attributes like height and muscle tone has led to even cis women being kicked out of women-only spaces). This is terrible for trans women and cis women alike.

Further, there have been repeated patterns of 'feminists' teaming up with groups that are incredibly anti-feminist to progress their transphobic efforts, all at the cost of women's rights. A relatively well-known

TERF group (which I won't name because they don't deserve any attention) that claims to fight for the rights of women has worked with conservative organisations numerous times. These collaborations include receiving donations from a Christian conservative group that opposes abortion.[1]

Despite the different attempts to create new names and groups (like TERFs and GCs), they're just transphobes and should be referred to as such. These particular transphobes like to miscommunicate truths about trans people, particularly trans women, because fundamentally, they don't see trans women as women. They wrongly view trans women as men invading women's spaces. Shaaba and I made an hour-long video unpacking GC transphobic arguments, which I've linked to in the Further Reading and Resources section of this book. We unpack a lot of the more frequent miscommunications in that video, and in the below myth-busting.

Myth: Trans rights oppose women's rights.

Wrong. As I've said before, **rights are not a pie**. Trans people, including trans women's rights, deserve to exist and be fought for as much as cis women's rights. In fact, trans women's rights and cis women's rights both fall under the category of women's rights. For example, women deserve protection against abuse by men,

---

1 'Far-Right Co-Option of the Transgender Rights Issue' (2019), Norris, *Byline Times* (https://bylinetimes.com/2021/09/30/the-far-right-co-option-of-the-transgender-rights-issue/)

and trans women are included in this. Women deserve freedom of choice over their bodies, and trans women are included in this. All women, trans or cis, should be advocating for all women's rights, equally.

Myth: Trans people accessing gendered spaces is dangerous, as trans women are a threat to cis women.

Wrong. It's a false and very dangerous belief that trans women are predatory, and that it's dangerous for them to be in the same spaces as cis women. If a trans woman escapes an abusive relationship, she deserves the support of a women's refuge. If a trans woman needs to use a toilet or changing room, she deserves to access women's toilets and changing rooms. Many regulatory bodies, safe space providers and the majority of society agree. **Trans people have been using spaces of their gender for a long time**, and are legally protected in doing so in the UK under the Equality Act. Bodies that govern refuges support trans women being in these spaces. They recognise that trans women need this support too, and pose no greater risk to cis women than other cis women.[1] In all this time, there has been no evidence that trans women have been a threat to cis women. Even if a case like this were to happen in the future, would it be right to restrict the access of an entire

1 'Potential Impacts of GRA Reform for Cisgender Women: Trans Women's Inclusion in Women-Only Spaces and Services' (2019), GRA EQIA Literature Search, Document 5

community because one person who'd shared that characteristic had happened to be a bad actor? There are many recorded instances of cis women inflicting violence in women-only spaces, so should all cis women therefore be banned from accessing them?

Unfortunately, by creating a lot of unnecessary fear around trans women, *all* women, including cis women, are being robbed of the support they deserve. This is because fewer efforts are being made to advocate against predatory men, which statistics show are the real cause of violence against women. By scapegoating trans women, GC transphobes are stopping the true feminist fight against dangerous men.

Myth: Trans men are confused lesbians who have been led astray by the allure of male privilege.

Wrong. I have to stop myself from laughing at this one. GC transphobes like to think of trans men as 'brainwashed' women who try to gain male privilege for an easier life. This again stems from the fact that they don't view trans men as men. This is particularly contradictory, because even if trans men were women – and we're not – you'd expect feminists to support them making their own decisions. Just another contradiction to GC transphobe thinking.

THE T IN LGBT

Myth: Reforming the Gender Recognition Act will endanger women.

Wrong. GC transphobes believe that a change to the Gender Recognition Act would allow trans people to access gendered spaces more easily. They think that a reform would endanger cis women because trans people (trans women specifically) would be able to self ID and gain access to women's spaces. The reality is, the proposed reforms to the Act have no impact on trans people's access to gendered spaces at all. Trans women are already legally allowed to access women's spaces under the Equality Act 2010. The Gender Recognition Act reform proposal would make it faster and cheaper for trans people to get a GRC (which pretty much only affects marriage, death and taxes). Once again: trans people don't need a GRC to access spaces of their gender; and more, it's actually illegal for a service or employer to ask trans people if they have one. I know, this particular GC transphobe reasoning makes *no* sense at all.

Myth: Children are too young to know they're trans.

Wrong. If this were the case, cis kids would also be too young to know they're cis, but we trust little girls when they say they're girls, and little boys when they say they're boys. Even very young children have a sense of gender, both their own and the gender of others, and both cis and trans kids have the ability to know who they are.

216

I had a sense of my gender from around four years old. I thought I was a boy, just like the other boys, and it wasn't until I was older that I noticed I was treated, and referred to, differently to other boys. Four-year-old me knew the truth all along.

☆ **Top Tip:** *Not everyone knows when they're young (more on this in a sec). There's no harm in allowing kids to express themselves how they feel comfortable.*

Myth: Children are being forced to transition and take medical steps that cause physical and irreversible changes.

Wrong. This is one of the most pervasive and damaging myths. No children are being forced to transition, or take irreversible hormone treatment, or have surgery. In fact, the reverse is true: trans children are often not believed when they tell people that they feel their gender differs from their assigned sex. Many parents reject their child's feelings or force them to express and present as their assigned sex.

Even if a child is supported by their family, there are a lot of steps and assessments involved in speaking to specialists. The affirming healthcare model is the accepted model, but for young children, gender-affirming care is all about supporting them in their expression, and a change of name and pronouns (the social elements of transitioning), as well as counselling. None of these steps involve irreversible physical changes to their body.

Even then, clinics that offer counselling for trans children are difficult to find. In the UK, only two clinics will speak with those who are under 18, and waiting lists are very long. Again, even still, hormones are **not** available to those under 16, and surgery is **not** available to those under 18. Once a child reaches puberty age, they may be able to access puberty blockers that temporarily pause puberty from taking place (and even this is likely to be inaccessible). After *all* of this, years of assessments, years of waiting, years of social transition, which allow trans people to know if this is right for them, hormones and surgery can be accessed at 16 and 18 respectively – and even still, the most common minimum age for hormones is 18 in the UK.[1]

So no, children are not having surgery or taking hormones, nor are they being forced to transition.

Myth: Most people go on to regret transitioning: de-transitioning rates are high.

Wrong. De-transitioning rates and regret rates are actually very low, with under 1 per cent of adult trans people de-transitioning.[2] Another longitudinal study found 97.5 per cent of kids who came out as trans still identify as trans five years later.[3]

---

1 Gender Identity Development Service: Puberty and physical intervention (https://gids.nhs.uk/young-people/puberty-and-physical-intervention/)
2 'Detransition Rates in a National UK Gender Identity Clinic' (2019), Davies, McIntyre and Rypma, *3rd Biennal EPATH Conference Inside Matters. On Law, Ethics and Religion*
3 'Gender Identity 5 Years After Social Transition' (2022), Olson, Durwood, Horton, Gallagher and Devor, *Pediatrics*

As with all numbers on a page, it's also important to look beyond them to the individual stories. The sad truth is that a lot of people who de-transition do so because it's unsafe for them to live as their true gender. They receive a lot of abuse, and determine that it's easier for them to present as their assigned sex. This isn't the case for everyone of course – sometimes people do genuinely de-transition – but the reported 1 per cent doesn't account for this difference.

Do you know what the regret rate is for medical procedures for non-trans-related surgeries? The plastic surgery regret rate was a whopping 65 per cent[1] – that's *significantly* higher than any trans-related procedures, where regret rates are described as exceedingly low.[2] But you can bet your bottom dollar that transphobes aren't campaigning for plastic surgery to stop.

It's not just the fault of transphobes: capitalist media outlets are also to blame for this scare. Headlines such as 'hundreds regret transitioning' deliberately aim to over-inflate the rate of de-transitioning. If they presented this as 100 in 10,000, or as under 1 per cent, there wouldn't be the same shock value, which would mean less incentive to click, and less traffic and revenue for their business bottom line. Media outlets don't care about the true de-transition rate. Nor do transphobes; they only want

---

1 'Do You Regret Having Cosmetic Surgery?', Medical Accident Group (https://www.medicalaccidentgroup.co.uk/news/do-you-regret-having-cosmetic-surgery/)
2 'Abstract: A Survey Study of Surgeons' Experiences with Regret and/ or Reversal of Gender-Confirmation Surgeries' (2018), Danker, Narayan, Bluebond-Langner et al., *Plastic and Reconstructive Surgery – Global Open*

to prevent trans people from accessing healthcare, and feel that de-transition scares could help incentivise their efforts.

Not only does this harm the trans community, it also harms those who de-transition. Once de-transitioners are used as sensationalist tactics to limit trans healthcare, they're often cast aside and are not provided with the support they truly need.

☆ **Top Tip:** *Sometimes the trans community can feel a lot of anger towards de-transitioners, but we should be treating them with the compassion and support that they need, and realise that transphobes and media outlets are the biggest weaponisers of the de-transition narrative. Trans people are the last community to force someone to pretend to be a gender that they're not!*

Some of the below myths don't necessarily come from a place of being transphobic, but from a place of simply not knowing. Even some trans people might begin their journeys believing these myths. Let's break these myths down.

Myth: All trans people want to transition the same.

Wrong. This myth is connected to the belief that there's such a thing as 'the surgery'. That transitioning is a one-stop sex-change procedure, and every trans person goes through the same cookie-cutter process, like Cybermen.

There's no single way to transition, and with many options in terms of social transition, hormones and surgeries, including not taking some of these steps, trans people rarely follow the exact same path.

Myth: Trans people are 'tricking' or 'fooling' others about their gender.

Wrong. If I was given a cake every time someone told me I'd 'fooled' them with my gender, I'd *almost* have enough cake to make up for the irritating comment. Sometimes this myth is presented from people innocently being taken aback by finding out you're trans. They'll say things like, 'I'd never be able to tell!' or, 'You had me fooled!' Even if it's coming from a good place, the connotations that trans people are trying to fool society feels uncomfortable and is fundamentally untrue.

Trans people are their gender (refer to busted myth #1). There's no tricking or fooling going on, because we're not pretending/trying to be something we're not.

Myth: Sexual orientation, gender identity and gender expression are all the same thing.

Wrong. These three concepts often get conflated, which contributes to a lot of the confusion around transness. Adding to this confusion, trans people's sexuality labels can be affected when they transition too, even if their attraction remains the same. For example, a trans man attracted to women may have identified as a lesbian before transitioning (hello!), and straight after he came out as trans. A further cherry of confusion can appear if trans people later discover a new sexuality for them after transitioning. Sometimes, the self-discovery and freedom of living as your true gender can lead you to discover other new aspects of your identity, including who you're attracted to.

With all these cherries and all this confusion, there is a simple way to think of it: your sexual orientation is about who you *like*, your gender is about who you know you *are*, and your gender expression is about how you *express*.

Myth: 'Transgender' is a gender.

Wrong. Transgender is an adjective, and trans is a prefix, not a separate gender. This confusion isn't helped by the fact that many forms (often well-meaningly!) have gender options of 'man', 'woman' and 'transgender'. I'm a tall man, and a man who wears glasses, but you don't see those as separate options on demographics surveys!

Many of these forms often erase non-binary identities too. The more we can raise awareness, understanding and education about T+ identities, the less these misconceptions will happen, and we're definitely making progress!

You Can Myth-Bust Too

It's great that I can give you a list of myths, explain why they're wrong and provide you with some references, but the real power is being able to myth-bust on your own. It's the whole 'don't give a man a fish, teach him how to fish and he'll never go hungry' (oops, I've made it deep again).

I'm not here to tell you what to think or who to believe. As a trans person, my aim is to happily live my life, and help other people like me to do the same. Like in the 'TERF Wars' essay breakdown video I made with Shaaba, all trans people and allies can do is provide information alongside points made by transphobes. It's up to you to decide what you want to believe, and what actions you choose to take from that.

To help you make **fully informed decisions**, I recommend you take time to research things before speaking about them publicly, make sure you check your sources are credible, and where possible:

Always try to find information from authentic sources.

If you're not sure what to believe about trans people, speak to the community directly. Listen to a bunch of their journeys, and then decide for yourself. I can't think of any context in which, if you were researching a topic, you wouldn't seek information from the actual community you were wanting to learn about.

💜 **For the Allies:** *Being the best ally isn't about blind loyalty to any person or any group. It's about doing your own research, and turning up to fully support a cause that you genuinely believe in. The best way to find out about anything is to go directly to the source. You wouldn't ask a white person to tell you* *what it's like to be brown – you'd speak to me! Similarly, you should listen to trans people (and a variety of them!) to understand their lived experiences, not transphobes. Take into account what other stakeholders are thinking, absolutely, and then come to your own conclusion. I guarantee you, listening to the humanised experiences of trans people will help you understand that the T+ community want to live as their true gender, nothing more, nothing less. – Shaaba*

12

THE NEVER-ENDING TRANSITION

The never-ending transition ... ah-ah-ahhh, ah-ah-ahhh, ah-ah-ahhhhh (I was going for the never-ending story theme there ...). My point is that transitioning can feel like a never-ending thing, a forever-stretching tunnel with an endpoint so far away you can barely see it.

Does it really end?

A common thought (though it's a huge misconception) is that a transition is 'over' when a trans person has 'the surgery' – yes, that pops up here too. There seems to be an assumption (like with transitioning being a one-stop surgery shop) that once you've had *that* surgery, you're all done. It's far more subjective than that, and some people don't have any surgery at all!

One way to think about it is that everyone is in a constant state of transition throughout their life in various different ways and contexts, and sometimes it's never to do with gender. We're always growing, we're always finding out who we are – and if you take HRT like me, you'll probably always be picking up those prescriptions, too.

To be annoying and wishy-washy, there are multiple different definitions of what people would consider an 'endpoint' to a transition, if there even is one. Yay, for clarity, ha-ha.

In the early days of my transition, my trans identity consumed a lot of my thoughts a lot of the time. It was exhausting. I constantly felt like I was fighting to reach the next step, desperate for a life after transitioning when I wouldn't have to think about it, and could just get on with the rest of my life. For me, each stage of transition that I passed meant less time focusing on being trans.

I *do* feel like my transition is over. I will always be trans, but I stopped transitioning once I'd completed all the trans-related things I needed to. Second-stage metoidioplasty felt so close to the endpoint, but it wasn't until I received my Gender Recognition Certificate and my new birth certificate that I truly felt my journey was complete. I hadn't decided in advance that this would be my end goal, it's just what felt right when it happened.

Receiving that GRC and my new birth certificate hit me harder than I expected. I felt such a big wave of relief. But realising that it marked the end of my transition for me didn't sink in straight away. Over the next few months, I noticed that I no longer felt anything hanging over me. There was no more waiting for an appointment letter, no more waiting for a phone call with a surgery date, no more gathering documents to prove that I was trans enough, no more waiting for strangers to decide if I deserved a new birth certificate. It was just all done.

There was nothing more I was waiting for, nothing more I needed.

I was finally content, happy and practically dysphoria-free (we'll circle back to this in a moment). The relief was REAL.

This endpoint can be so subjective because not everyone has the same transition steps in their journey, and not everyone transitions in one go. Like with a lot of things in life, it's all about the individual. Some people don't feel there's an endpoint at all, as hormones are often a lifelong commitment. I personally don't see this as part of me being trans, but just part of me getting older. That might sound a bit weird, but hormones will continue causing changes for a very long time, as they do in cis people too. Sure, the testosterone in my body will see me getting progressively hairier (I swear I'm six months away from having shoulder hair I could plait), but that would be the case if I were cis too.

Circling back to dysphoria, as promised, I want to mention that you can feel 'done' with your transition and still have gender dysphoria. There might be things you're dysphoric about that can't be changed by hormones, surgery or socially transitioning – and that's okay. I still have some moments where dysphoria pokes its ugly head up to say hello. It's incredibly rare, but not unheard of. Transitioning does greatly reduce gender dysphoria for trans people, but it's not guaranteed that it will go away completely. This doesn't mean that your transition has failed; it just can't always solve everything trans people might be dysphoric about.

In conclusion, transitioning doesn't have to be never-ending, but there's no right or wrong answer, or moment for it to feel 'done'. Just like there's no deadline for coming out, there's no pressure to set a deadline to finish your transition either.

WHEN (IF EVER) WILL YOU CONSIDER YOUR TRANSITION TO BE COMPLETE?

'I will consider my transition complete the day I'm comfortable with who I am, the day I can confidently look in the mirror and be happy with who I see. Obviously I'm human, so there will still be bad days. But I know that little me would be so proud if he knew that the good days dominate, and that's what I'm going for.'

Leander, 18, trans man

'I think every human, cis or transgender, is in some kind of transition their entire life. So I do not think my transition will ever be complete and I am 100 per cent okay with that.'

Lesley, 30, genderqueer/non-binary

'For now, I consider that my transition will be complete once I have my top surgery.'

Dante, 29, trans man

'I think I will feel that my transition is complete once I have metoidioplasty. But I don't know. I think this might be a forever journey.'

Graysen, 29, trans man

You're More than Your Transness

There's such a pervasive message coming from media (mainstream media specifically) that trans people are only interesting because they're trans. In all the documentaries, news stories, TV appearances and even across many fictional TV shows and movies, trans people are almost always depicted as two-dimensional walking, talking vessels of transness. More specifically, we're often depicted at our lowest: the bullying, the struggling, the conflict, the non-acceptance.

What we rarely see, and truly NEED, is passive trans representation.

Like, hey, a person who likes reading, or playing football, or singing, or cooking. Oh, and they also happen to be trans.

Because of this lack of passive representation, when I was earlier on in my transition, I honestly felt like my life would always be about the fact that I was trans. It made sense at the time, as all the steps I had taken, was taking, and was excited to take took up a lot of headspace, emotional energy and actual time. The truth is, there are so many other parts of my life that I love exploring. My relationships, my hobbies, my studies – my cats!

☆ **Top Tip:** *Taking the time to nurture the other dimensions of you can not only help with your development, but also help make time feel faster and more productive as you're progressing with your transition. It's all useful, because it's all helping to build the real you.*

IN WHAT WAYS ARE YOU MORE THAN YOUR TRANS IDENTITY?

'I am a doctor, I play sports, I am a concert pianist.'

Charlie, 28, woman (trans woman/intersex)

'I'm a parent. I'm also an artist, a creator, an activist and a writer.'

Anon., 37, non-binary/trans masc

'All my being is trans but being trans isn't all I am.'

Rowen, 18, trans man/masc

'Me being trans doesn't change that I am a person.'

Victor, 20, trans man

'I have conducted operas, symphonies and film scores with incredible musicians in incredible places. I volunteer with the RSPB and the RSPCA. I love movies and art and books'

Jamie, 20, trans man

'Being trans has been a colour in my life, but it is far from the whole picture.'

Daniel, 19, trans man

'I'm pansexual, a brother to my younger siblings, a boyfriend, a student and a cat-dad. I'm study-ing art therapy hoping to become a psychologist in the future. I'm ambitious and want to change the psychology of how labels affect our lives, and improve therapy methods.'

Louis, 24, trans man

'I am a cat-dad, an adoptee, an advocate, a musician and a person who loves/cares deeply for others.'

Sanjay, 30, transgender man

'I am queer, Jewish, mixed race; I love music and I'm a writer; I have a full-time job and a partner. My life revolves around everything else ... and I can go for weeks at a time without even thinking, *Huh, I'm trans.* Now I have transitioned, I can simply "be".'

Jonathan, 30, trans man

'I am disabled, I am neurodivergent, I am queer, I am a poet, a student, and a friend.'

River, 21, trans man

'I'm a nerd, support worker, mental health and diversity advocate, bookworm, nurturing cat-loving person and friend.'

Milo, 24, trans man

To Be or Not to Be (an Activist)?

One way that trans identities constantly feel front and centre, even after a transition seems complete, is in the constant need to fight for our right to exist. Gripping that shield of trans affirmation and picking up that anti-transphobia poking stick can feel like a full-time job sometimes.

Unfortunately, there is a lot of transphobia in the world, online and offline, and often it feels like it's never-ending. This isn't something you or any other trans person deserves to experience, and there is no good reason for people to be transphobic. But saying this doesn't make it go away. The lingering stink of transphobia makes it important for all trans people to know how to deal with it, and how to protect their own mental health, both during and after transitioning.

The first thing to remember is that for every transphobe that exists in the world, there are even more allies. What transphobes don't want you to know is that they're a small minority that like to shout very loud, and whenever they do shout, all you need to do is turn your head the other way. I guarantee you that for every transphobic protest group of a handful of people outside a Primark, there are significantly more allies showing trans support.

And there is always support out there. From friends and family to support groups and online spaces, having supportive people in your life, and knowing that you are accepted and respected, can help so much. Focus on these positive connections, and wherever possible, avoid those that bring you nothing but negativity.

This leads nicely onto the next point about not being an activist, and this one might feel closer to home. It's easier said than done (and sometimes may feel truly impossible), but when you feel ready, it's important to cut toxic people and places out of your life. Being an activist means protecting your individual right to survive and thrive, as well as your community.

You never need to keep someone in your life who doesn't accept you, respect you or treat you the way you deserve to be treated – no matter who they are.

Toxic spaces can be easier to cut out than people, and can still make a big positive impact. There's a lot of transphobia online, for example: people are much more likely to be openly transphobic when they can hide behind a screen, anonymously or not. That way, they don't actually have to say their hate to people's faces, or be called out in person. Taking a break from social media sites or stopping use of them completely is a great way to protect your mental health.

You don't need to fight everywhere, all the time.

Sometimes I feel overwhelmed by the loudness of the negativity towards the trans community, and it can really get me down to be constantly exposed to this negativity. Whenever I'm feeling like transphobia is getting too much, I step away from places like Twitter and focus on non-trans-related things in my life. I see friends, explore new places with my wife, read a book, eat some pizza, build some Lego – all the things that make me happy, and all the other things that make me *me*. It's like a little refresh, and I can come back feeling like my defences have been rebuilt.

💜 **For the Allies:** *I can get infuriated by transphobic news, but as an ally I can also detach myself from it. It's important to remember that for trans people, transphobia isn't just an academic exercise. It's a deeply personal attack that we'll never be able to fully relate to as allies. Consider your trans loved one's state of mind before sharing trans news, especially if it's negative. And when your trans loved one needs to take a break, that's the perfect time to lend your support to trans causes. Vote, sign petitions, speak up and attend Prides and protests if you feel it's safe to do so. And as for your trans loved one, support them by taking part in their lives beyond their trans identity (that's if Jamie lets me anywhere near the Lego!).* – Shaaba

Sometimes I only come back because it's related to my job. If I didn't make content calling out transphobia, I'd probably stay away from certain platforms permanently. So don't feel like you ever *have* to go back – I'm still trying to take my own advice here!

*Trans lives and bodies are politicised
so much by others.*

It creates this pressure and false belief that if you're trans you automatically have to be an activist. But you don't have to be involved in every political update, or be up-to-date on every piece of trans-related news, good or bad. It's a given that you deserve a life without transphobia,

THE NEVER-ENDING TRANSITION

but as that's unrealistic, let me also say:

> *You deserve to live a life of free choice,*
> *including walking away from the trans*
> *fight whenever you need to.*

There's nothing wrong with doing this. You're not letting anyone down.

THE HAPPY ENDING

Ha-ha-ha. This is me laughing because there's a bit of innuendo to the title of this chapter. I hope it made you laugh too (or at least smile!), because that's exactly what this chapter is about: the happiness, pride and euphoria that only being trans can bring.

If you pay too much attention to the news or watch certain movies and TV shows, it's likely that you've been given the impression that being trans is all doom, gloom, misery, turmoil, sadness, [insert all the other negative adjectives you can think of here].

It really isn't all doom and gloom.

There are of course difficulties that come with being trans. There are tough times, and sad times, and it's important to not downplay these. If I could magically have the same life that I have right now but be cis, I'd be stupid not to take it and remove all the dysphoria and discrimination. But – a big but – none of that erases the fact that there also funny, joyful, light-hearted moments about being trans. Moments that push back against the stereotype that trans people are just walking, talking vessels of suffering and sadness.

This portrayal of being trans having a lighter side to it, and a less invasive side that doesn't take up your whole identity, is a big part of why I continue to create online. (Well, that and education through entertainment – we've got to show how wrong those transphobes are every now and again!)

I want to share some of those hilariously awkward moments that have brought me a lot of laughs in my life, that wouldn't have happened if I wasn't trans.

Now, I've already said I'm a trans guy who didn't use a packer, but I did own one for a short period of time. An extra-small Mr Limpy, just in case you were curious. (It was plenty big enough, also just in case you were curious!) I wore it a couple of times and hid it somewhere. I say 'somewhere', because I *literally still to this day, a decade later, have no idea where it is.* I was living at my parents' place, and I'd read one too many embarrassing stories about people leaving their packers for others to find, and then I did that thing where I clearly hid it too well (facepalm). When I moved out, I thought I'd find it again. Nope. I'm also 99.7 per cent confident I didn't throw it away. I just can't believe there's a squishy willy sitting at my parents' house and they could come across it at any moment – or maybe they already have!

I also mentioned going to university. One of my lecturers asked me about my dissertation project, and I explained I was interested in studying trans wellbeing. He gave me a book he thought I'd find useful. It was terrible, so I won't promote the title or author, and he had no idea how harmful the book was for the trans community, but I was so confused that I'd been given this, as it was all about trans women. Many years later, the lecturer confessed he'd given it to me because he'd thought I was a trans woman at the beginning of my journey, not realising I was a trans guy who'd already started transitioning! The whole thing was quite affirming and amusing.

A final story I'll share with you (I'm slightly concerned these are only funny to me because I was there, ha-ha) involved me (about three months on T), Shaaba and our friend at college. We were sitting in an empty classroom during a break and Shaaba randomly started singing the lyrics to 'The Lion Sleeps Tonight'. No idea why. Our friend joined in with the 'a-wimoweh's, and I was gearing up to join in with the 'a-wee-ee-ee', but as I did, my voice broke so badly. We laughed so much that day, and they teased me for months, calling me a squeaky chicken (Shaaba still brings it up sometimes to this day)! I did sound like a squeaky chicken, to be honest.

> **DO YOU HAVE ANY FUNNY OR HAPPY MOMENTS TO SHARE THAT HAVE ONLY HAPPENED BECAUSE YOU'RE TRANS?**
>
> 'Me and my sister were playing a game where you guess words. My sister was explaining the word "braces" and said, "You had these removed," and I screamed, "TITTIES!" and we almost died laughing and Mom had to come check on us.'
>
> *Alice, 21, trans man*

'A friend once forgot I am transgender and asked whether me and my twin brother are identical. I then reminded her, and we still laugh about it.'

Daniel, 19, trans man

'Being filmed for the Channel 4 documentary *The Boy Who Was Born a Girl* in 2009 was an important moment – it catalogued my early transition as well as sharing a first-hand account of a trans teenager growing up, which was one of the first positive depictions in the UK mainstream media of young trans people. It makes me happy that in some way I have inspired others to discover their own trans identities and to live as their authentic selves.'

Jonathan, 30, trans man

'Having a trans flag pin on my bag has brought about many impactful moments where relative strangers will come up to me and tell me how safe they felt when I was around in a class, at an event, etc. Or I would be the first person they felt comfortable to come out to.'

Rowen, 18, trans man/masc

'I was at the back of the bus on my way home from my third stage of phallo. My erectile device had been put in, which basically meant I had to travel home with an erection as part of my recovery, and unfortunately the tracksuit bottoms I'd thought would help conceal it weren't doing a very good job. An older lady came and sat down next to me on the bus. She did a double take at my erection and had no idea where to look!'

Finlay, 48, trans man

Finding Trans Joy

The final thing I want to have a chat about is trans joy. I've not just made that up, it's a real term that describes trans people claiming their identity and celebrating who they are, rather than feeling shame.

Trans people can, and most definitely do, find joy and happiness!

This doesn't have to be at the 'end' of your transition either; this can be in the small moments, the big moments and all the moments in between, before, during and after (if you feel there is an after) your transition!

Trans joy is showing that being trans is not a sentence of misery, or of being unsuccessful. It shows that trans people are people in this world doing their thing, living their lives, with every capability and possibility of achieving dreams, being successful, finding love, raising plants, pets and kids, finding happiness and being content with who they are.

I've met so many wonderful people in my life because I'm trans. I found a comfort and contentment in who I am throughout my transition. I've had moments of joy the first time I left the house with a new haircut, hearing my voice breaking (despite the mild to moderate embarrassment), getting my first beard hair, receiving my new birth certificate ... I could honestly go on and on.

Trans people's lives are as full and as meaningful as anyone else's.

WHAT IS TRANS JOY TO YOU?

'Trans joy is what keeps me going. It's the feeling of absolute euphoria, like the first time you could actually look in the mirror and recognise yourself, recognise the person you are fighting to become.'

Leander, 18, trans man

'I'd say it's those wins in an otherwise uphill battle. Those moments when you can sit back and see how far you've come, and realise that the person in the mirror is starting to look like you.'

George, 18, trans man

'It is peace. It is the absence of pain. It is being free.'

Charlie, 28, woman (trans woman/intersex)

'Just celebrating and basking in the euphoria of being yourself and allowing yourself to break the mould made for you.'

Eve, 26, trans woman

'Feeling absolute happiness at being trans and the connectedness with the community.'

Asher, 23, AFAB non-binary

'It's one of the most beautiful things I've ever seen: it's when a person who has life so much more diffi-cult, just because of who they are, finds something that makes those problems feel insignificant.'

Amity, 18, trans woman

> 'Trans joy means unapologetic and genuine freedom of expression. Existing and being proud of what I have to offer the world – knowing my worth and accepting my journey!'
>
> *Theo, 27, trans masc/non-binary*

In many ways, I'm grateful to be trans. It's not a turd I need to polish, it's just a different way of being, and it's brought me so many things that I otherwise might not have had or experienced.

I never would have become friends with Shaaba, as she wasn't allowed to be friends with boys, ha-ha, so that's already a major win for being trans. I have a more open mind about the whole world because of my transness. While I wouldn't choose the hardships that comes with being trans, I'm very grateful for my chosen family, who I've only had the privilege of meeting because we're part of the same community. Writing this book, doing a job that I love, meeting amazing and inspiring people and travelling the world - these are all things that have happened as a direct result of me being trans, and talking about it.

Maybe some of these things might have happened in a slightly different way even if I wasn't trans, but that's not the life I'm living, and I wouldn't risk what I have now for what-ifs.

Until Next Time

I want to thank you so much for reading this book, it's been such a journey writing it. I've cried happy tears, and sad tears. I've felt so much hope that things are getting better, and so much solidarity with how tough things still are. There's clearly still a *long* way to go for trans rights. Most importantly, I've been reminded of the true joy and peace that being trans, and being able to transition, has brought to my life. Whatever your reason for picking this book up, I hope you were able to embrace all sorts of feelings too, and can close it having learnt more about yourself, the trans experience or how to be an ultimate supportive ally – perhaps you've even learnt a combination of these things!

Wherever you're at in your journey, no matter how difficult things have been, or currently are, know that you deserve to experience peace and happiness in your identity, and you will! You deserve acceptance, respect and to live life as your true self. Surround yourself with people who support you with this, and know that if you ever need me, I'll also be on my channel, cheering you on from the side-lines as you go through this epic journey!

You are loveable, you are amazing, and being trans never has to hold you back.

And *that's* the real T.

Acknowledgements

Writing a book has been a lifelong ambition, and to have written something that can hopefully help my community makes achieving this goal feel even more special. Although my name is on the cover, I didn't create this on my own, and doing so would have been impossible. Many incredible people have been a part of this process, and I want to take a moment to thank them too.

I'd like to extend thanks to Penguin Random House and 84 World for this opportunity, particularly Jenny, Evangeline and Sam.

This book would also not have been possible without the support and contributions from the trans community. It's a community with so much love and understanding, and it's a community I am genuinely proud to be a part of. Thank you to everyone who has taken the time to share their stories for this book, and to everybody more generally who has supported and been a part of my journey online. You've helped me feel less alone, and have changed my life in more ways than one.

I'd also like to thank the people in my life who have helped me in my own transition journey, without whom I wouldn't be in a position to help others. The trans people who shared their stories and helped me not only realise my identity, but accept and embrace it. And the loved ones in my life, particularly my parents, whose support means the world to me.

Finally, a massive thank-you to my wife, Shaaba, who has been by my side from the beginning of my journey. My best friend, and my partner in love, life and everything. From never making a mistake with my pronouns, to staying up until 4am helping me with this book (on more than one occasion!), thank you. I couldn't have done any of this without you – and by 'this' I mean my transition, and particularly this book!

Further Reading
and Resources

If you haven't already, I would highly recommend reading, watching and looking into multiple resources, not just one or two. Especially if you're figuring yourself out/in the very early stages of transition, or if you're an ally wanting to learn more. I hope my book has been somewhat helpful, but it's definitely not the only thing you should be looking at. It's always important to be as informed as possible before forming a plan or opinion. A huge part of humanising and learning more about trans people is to be aware of a variety of perspectives and hear the voices of multiple people too, so I've compiled a list of books, people and more that I found particularly helpful, or that members of the trans community have recommended to me.

There are loads of amazing books from different perspectives, from memoirs, to historical compilations about trans history, to fiction, but here are a few that I would recommend:

- *Trans Mission: My Quest to a Beard* by Alex Bertie

- *Sorted: Growing Up, Coming Out, and Finding My Place* by Jackson Bird

- *The Transgender Issue: An Argument for Justice* by Shon Faye

- *Welcome to St. Hell* by Lewis Hancox

- *To My Trans Sisters* edited by Charlie Craggs

- *Trans Britain: Our Journey From the Shadows* edited by Christine Burns

- *In Their Shoes: Navigating Non-Binary Life* by Jamie Windust

- *Yes, You Are Trans Enough: My Transition From Self-Loathing to Self-Love* by Mia Violet

- *Transgender History* by Susan Stryker

- *Top to Bottom: A Memoir and Personal Guide Through Phalloplasty* by Finlay Games

- *None of the Above: Reflections on Life Beyond the Binary* by Travis Alabanza

If one book is enough for now or you want another medium to explore, here are some cool trans people who are out there living their visible lives on social media, who would be great to give a follow to:

- Kenny-Ethan Jones
  @kennyethanjones

- Juno Dawson
  @junodawson

- Munroe Bergdorf
  @munroebergdorf

- Elliot Page
  @elliotpage

- Gottmik
  @gottmik

- Noah Adams
  @noahfinnce

- Shone Faye
  @shon.faye

- Charlie Craggs
  @charlie_craggs

- Lewis Hancox
  @lewishancoxfilms

- Jackson Bird
  @jackisnotabird

- Janet Mock
  @janetmock

- Paris Lees
  @paris.lees

- Jamie Windust
  @jamie_windust

- Veronica Blades
  @missxronix

- Finlay Games
  @finntheinfinncible

- Luxeria
  @xxluxeria

- Travis Alabanza
  @travisalabanza

- Alex Bertie
  @therealalexbertie

- Shivani Dave
  @day_vey

- Jazz Jennings
  @jazzjennings_

- Shane Ortega

- Hannah Graf
  @hannahw253

- Jake Graf
  @jake_graf5

- Laverne Cox
  @lavernecox

- Chella Man
  @chellaman

- Yasmin Finney
  @yazdemand

- Zach Barack
  @zachbarack

- Kayden Coleman
  @kaydenxofficial

- Indya Moore
  @indyamoore

- Sam Smith
  @samsmith

- MJ Rodriguez
  @mjrodriguez7

- Kim Petras
  @kimpetras

- Thomas Beatie
  @thomassecretstory10

- Asia Kate Dillon

- Kye Allums

- Georgina Beyer

Then away from these amazing individual people, there are also trans-specific or very trans-helpful charities and websites that you can check out:

- Mermaids: https://mermaidsuk.org.uk

- The Trevor Project: https://www.thetrevorproject.org

- Gendered Intelligence: https://genderedintelligence. co.uk

- Gender Identity Research & Education Society (GIRES): https://www.gires.org.uk

- Gender Minorities Aotearoa: https://genderminorities. com

- Not A Phase: https://notaphase.org

- The Small Trans Library in Dublin and Glasgow: https:// smalltranslibrary.org/

Other Resources

Gender dysphoria symptoms:

https://www.mayoclinic.org/diseases-conditions/gender-dysphoria/symptoms-causes/syc-20475255

https://www.nhs.uk/conditions/gender-dysphoria/ symptoms/

Where to find gender-neutral toilets:
https://www.refugerestrooms.org/

Further reading for hormone changes:

https://www.gendergp.com/hrt-timelines-hormones-effects/

Breaking down J.K. Rowling's 'TERF Wars' essay:
https://www.youtube.com/watch?v=6Avcp-e4bOs

BBC Asian Network study:
https://www.bbc.co.uk/news/uk-45133717

Research Papers and References

You also may have noticed some footnotes throughout the book. If you want to get your science on and dive into some of the topics further, here are some references:

The Role of Gender Affirmation in Psychological Well-Being among Transgender Women (2016) Glynn et. al., APA; Effects of Testosterone Treatment and Chest Reconstruction Surgery on Mental Health and Sexuality in Female-to-Male Transgender People (2014) Davies & Colton Meier, International Journal of Sexual Health;

Evidence Supporting The Biological Nature of Gender Identity (20115) Saraswat, Weinand, & Safer, Endocrine Practice

Sexual Differentiation of The Human Brain: Relation to Gender Identity, Sexual Orientation, and Neuropsychiatric Disorders (2011) Bao & Swaab, Frontiers in Neuroendocrinology

Male-to-Female Transsexuals Have Female Neuron Numbers in The Limbic Nucleus (2000) Kruijver et. al., The Journal of Clinical Endocrinology and Metabolism

Patterns of Genital Sexual Arousal in Transgender Men (2021) Raines et. al., Association for Psychological Science

Mental Health Outcomes in Transgender and Nonbinary Youths Receiving Gender-Affirming Care (2022) Tordoff, Wanta, & Collin et. al., JAMA Network Open; Pubertal Suppression for Transgender Youth and Risk of Suicidal Ideation (2022) Turban, King, Carswell, & Keuroghlian, PEADIATRICS.

Gender Identity Development Service *Puberty and Physical Intervention* Accessed January 2023 (https://gids.nhs.uk/young-people/puberty-and-physical-intervention/)

Sian Norris, Byline Times, 2019, The Far-Right Co-option of The Transgender Rights Movement, Accessed January 2023 (https://bylinetimes.com/2021/09/30/the-far-right-co-option-of-the-transgender-rights-issue/)

Potential Impacts of GRA Reform for Cisgender Women: Trans Women's Inclusion in Women-Only Spaces and Services (2019) GRA EQIA Literature search Document 5.

Gender Identity Development Service *Puberty and Physical Intervention* Accessed January 2023 (https://gids.nhs.uk/young-people/puberty-and-physical-intervention/)

Detransition Rates In a National UK Gender Identity Clinic (2019) Davies, McIntyre, & Rypma, 3rd Biennal EPATH Conference Inside Matters. On Law, Ethics, and Religion

Gender Identity 5 Years after Transition (2022) Olson, Durwood, Horton, Gallagher, & Devor, PEDIATRICS

Do You Regret Having Surgery? The Medical Accident Group, Accessed January 2023, https://www. medicalaccidentgroup.co.uk/news/do-you-regret-having-cosmetic-surgery/#:~:text=Research%20by%20 Medical%20Accident%20Group,form%20of%20 cosmetic%20procedure%20again.

Abstract: A Survey Study of Surgeon's Experiences with Regret and/or Reversal of Gender-Confirmation Surgeries (2018) Danker, Narayan, & Bluebond-Langer et. al., Plastic and Reconstructive Surgery-Global Open

Helplines

Finally – but very importantly – if you, or someone you know, could do with some support and aren't sure where to find it, here are some links to updated helplines resources from all over the world.

Together We Are Strong: https://togetherweare-strong. tumblr.com/helpline

Directory of International Mental Health Helplines: https://www.helpguide.org/articles/therapy-medication/ directory-of-international-mental-health-helplines.htm

Never feel afraid to ask for help. You deserve it, and support *is* out there, I promise!

INDEX

INDEX